KU-289-415

DISTRICT 13 OF MEDELLÍN
The Drama of the Armed Conflict

YONI ALEXANDER RENDÓN RENDÓN

DISTRICT  OF MEDELLÍN
The Drama of the Armed Conflict

Pulso & Letra
Editores

ISBN: 978-958-46-8996-2
© Yoni Alexander Rendón Rendón
E-mail: bookdistrict13ofmedellin@gmail.com
📞 + 57 312 266 9668

Translation by: Interpreters and Translations an X Group Company, Envigado, Colombia.

Book Cover by: The X Group

Translation reviewed by: Heriberto Rivera, Juan Camilo Echeverry Bedoya, Herly Ibarguen Murillo, Luis Hernando Murillo, Jayanth Padmakumar, Smith Vargas Roa, Freddy Aparicio, Oscar Mauricio Graciano López, Alejandro Zapata Hoyos, Caittin Sylk, Ángela María Restrepo Acevedo, Uday Unzaga Acuña, Luis Horacio Tejada Holguín, Cesar Calonge Sáez, Tim Dowling, David Hernández Quintero, Luisa Fernanda Castaño Santa, Orlando Jiménez, Paula Villegas Correa and Mauricio Ortiz Echavarría.

Printed and made in Colombia

Copyright: The copyrighted portions of this book may not be reproduced or transmitted in any form or by any means, electronic or mechanical including photocopying, recording, by any information storage and retrieval system, without permission in writing from the publisher.

Acknowledgements

This book is dedicated to my mother Marleny del Socorro Rendón R, for her constant support in good and bad times.

Also to Luis Carlos Pérez Villa, Alonso Salazar Jaramillo, Carolina Gómez Salazar, Alirio Antonio Machado, Heriberto Rivera, Fabian Ruiz Velasquez, Juan Camilo Echeverry Bedoya, Luis Horacio Tejada Holguín, Alexis Espinosa, Fabián Ruiz Velásquez, Cesar Calonge Sáez, Smith Vargas Roa, Luis Hernando Murillo, Freddy Aparicio, Herly Ibarguen, Jayanth Padmakumar, Caittin Sylk, Ángela María Restrepo Acevedo, Uday Unzaga Acuña, Tim Dowling, Gerardo Posada Cadavid, Orlando Jiménez, Johan Granada, Mauricio Ortiz Echavarría, Luisa Fernanda Castaño Santa, Oscar Mauricio Graciano Lopez, Andrés Galeano, Carolina Cadavid Vargas, Jorge Martínez Flores, Dora Ligia Bueno Becerra, Alejandro Zapata, Jerson Herrera, Gloria Ocampo, Manuel López, William Díaz, Milly Díaz, María Cecilia Callejas, Paula Villegas Correa, Fernando Osorio, Robinson Úsuga, Eduardo Cano Bustamante, Ángela María Quintero, Vanesa Fonnegra, Eugenia Margarita Sánchez, Mónica Restrepo, Ricardo Alfonso Ocampo, Juan Estevan Gallón, Lucila Amparo Céspedes, María Edilia Tascón, Claudia Patricia Zapata, Patricia Elena Palacio, Andrea Palacio Zapata, Uriel Calle, Eduardo Paniagua, Wilinton Foronda, Juan Bautista Zapata, Luz Nasly García, Sonia Maria Bedoya, Adriana Maria Mazo, Lázaro Correa Rodríguez, Bertha Inés Gómez, Marta Cecilia Gómez, Guillermo Molina, Mario Castrillón, Roberto Seguín, Rafael Orlando Jaramillo and David Hernández Quintero.

Also to the Colombian National Police, Canadian School, Alejandro Vélez Barrientos School, Colombo British College and Diamond Graphics Company.

And to those people who even though they have not been mentioned for different reasons, have one way or another helped to make this book a reality.

Content

Preface

By Alonso Salazar Jaramillo
The former Mayor of Medellín City 2008-2011.

On October 16th, 2002, when President Alvaro Uribe ordered the military to go in and take over Comuna 13, my niece Carolina Gomez was being held captive there. Her testimony about how she was taken, what happened while she was being held captive and how she was rescued, became one of the stories compiled by Yoni Alexander Rendon in his book *Area 13 Medellín, The Drama of the Armed Conflict*.

Yoni Alexander is a community police officer. When I was appointed Government Secretary of Medellín, I was pleasantly surprised to see that the community police team was made up of people with deep rooted social, artistic and literary knowledge. I was able to get closer and learn more about Alirio Antonio Machado and Yoni Rendon. When Officer Rendon found out about my consanguinity with Carolina, he looked me up and asked me to read his manuscript.

Yoni is a humble man, who besides being serious about his writing, is recognized for his ability to work inside communities that have suffered the impact of sustained periods of violence, such as the northeast zone of Medellín and Comuna 13.

Regarding his book about Comuna 13, Yoni Rendón, through testimonies and psychological analysis, has described the history of this area of Medellín, which has suffered an acute background of violence, poverty and neglect. Comuna 13 was repeatedly subject to terror caused by criminal gangs, guerillas and paramilitary groups.

11

The FARC, ELN and CAP, subjected the community to their will for over ten years, through the use of violence and crime. Rendon talks about how these armed groups cruelly murdered youth, displaced families, created deadly borders, kidnapped public officials working in the area, placed fragmentation grenades under the corpses of their victims to kill criminalists and police officers who were called on to process crime scenes, and even killed each other over territorial control. He also talks about how those rebels had expanded their criminal action with a large number of kidnappings citywide. He mentions several people: a public employee was kidnapped with his family, some INPEC officials, and a dentist. These are just a brief sample of the hundreds of people who were victims in Medellín.

The text also describes how the conflict in Comuna 13 worsened after the year 2000, because that is when the paramilitary groups started fighting against the urban guerillas to take control over these territories. The battles resulted in the death of residents of buildings in the area and even people from relatively distant neighborhoods who were struck in the privacy of their own homes by stray ammunition from long-range weapons.

Carolina, my niece, was kidnapped at 5:30 in the morning on her way to class at the university. By mere coincidence, at the time she was kidnapped, the military operation Orion, which focused on getting government forces to go in and retake the area by force and defeat the guerilla groups, had already been set in motion.

Carolina explains everything that happened step by step. She describes the gloomy, dark and smelly room which she was taken to, but especially focuses on describing her captors, people dragged into extreme circumstances at a very young age (even 15 years old), who could hardly be aware of the 'ideology' they were defending. She narrates the terror she felt during the continuous battles which lasted several days in order to retake Comuna 13, her horror at seeing corpses on the stairways when they moved her from hideout to hideout, and her arrival at a house where two militants lay dead on the floor, as well as how the Gaula police team came into the last house where she was being held to rescue her.

The military operation Orion caused controversy and was questioned by some people, but it is remembered by Carolina and the inhabitants of Comuna 13 as redemption.

Yoni Rendón is committed to making sure that the history of Comuna 13 is never forgotten. He wants to ensure that people from Medellín are well aware that not long ago large sectors of the city were at the will of powerful illegal forces. People must know that this situation was perceived with indifference for many years because the people who were living through it, were the poorest dwellers of the city, as in the case of Comuna 13 and that this situation had to affect the middle and upper classes, in order for it to become an important issue for everyone.

President Uribe gave the order and changed the history of Comuna 13 of Medellín. The military operation Orion marked the beginning of the end of the guerilla's territorial control inside the city. After this, the other part of the conflict –the paramilitary groups - demobilized.

When Sergio Fajardo was the Mayor of Medellín City, his administration implemented a new strategy of security and community living; this helped decrease the crime rate. But there is a long way to go. Overcoming this kind of history has not been easy and will not be in the future either. We know that in order for the city to progress, illegal forces cannot be allowed to take on the government's role. Personal safety is a right that must be guaranteed to all citizens, starting with the poorest, who have been affected the most by violence and insecurity.

MAP OF MEDELLIN CITY DEMARCATED BY COMUNAS

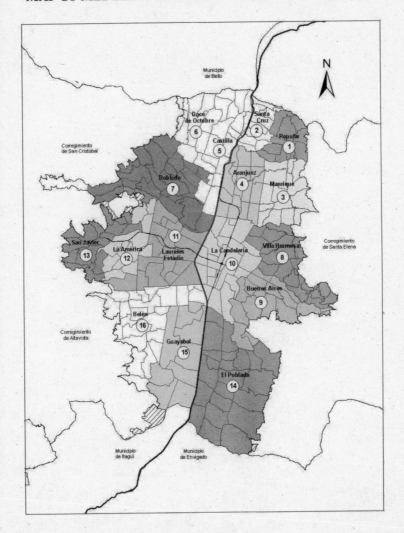

Map: Courtesy of Sub-Direction Metro – Municipal Planning Information. Government of Medellín.

MAP OF COMUNA 13 DEMARCATED BY NEIGHBORHOODS

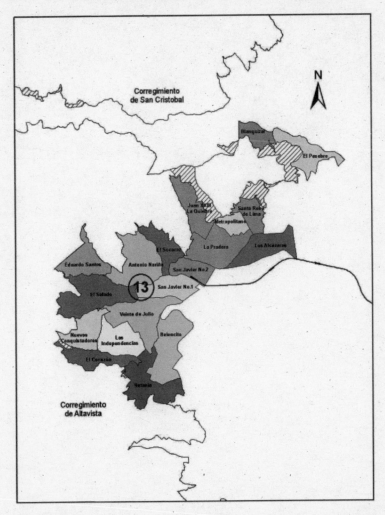

Map: Courtesy of Sub-Direction Metro – Municipal Planning Information. Government of Medellín.

Brief History and Introduction

Comuna 13 in Medellín city is made up of the following neighborhoods: Veinte de Julio, El Salado, Nuevos Conquistadores, Las Independencias, El Corazón, Belencito, Betania, El Pesebre, Blanquizal, Santa Rosa de Lima, Los Alcázares, Metropolitano, La Pradera, Juan XXIII-La Quiebra, Antonio Nariño, San Javier I y II, Eduardo Santos and El Socorro. These neighborhoods take up an area of seven square kilometers.

In the late seventies, families from other sectors of the city, who did not have homes, began to move to some areas of Comuna 13. After that, families displaced by violence from other regions of Antioquia and even from Choco started coming to Comuna 13 under the same conditions. These people built their homes with materials such as wood, plastic, clay, cardboard, zinc roof sheets, aluminum cans or bamboo. Because of the lack of potable water, they would take advantage of the water springs in the mountains and would carry the water through hoses to the nearest dwellings. Since there were no sewers, they would build ditches on the side of the mountain in order to evacuate the sewage. To cook, first, they used stoves with firewood and subsequently installed illegal power connections by using wired extensions from the surrounding areas where there were power poles, thus bringing the energy all the way to their living areas.

Many people in this area had not yet even solved some of the most urgent needs of public services, when they began to be intimidated by criminal gangs that were emerging and taking control of most of the territory. The members of these gangs committed all kinds of abuses against the population, such as theft, extortion, assaults, threats and rapes. According to Ms. Mery, who was one of the first residents of Las Independencias neighborhood, "In the neighborhood they stole a lot; if you had a small pot in the kitchen with food, they would steal the pot even with what was cooking in it."

"The nature of invasion that characterized [sic] the history of the western central area regains a bigger significance nowadays when analyzing social realities experienced by its inhabitants. On one hand, to its never-ending story of shortages of all kinds, we can add the social fragmentation caused by high levels of violence, stemming from the armed conflict that raged even more intensely in that area of the city; and on the other hand, its topographical, political, cultural, social and economic classification, emphasize the characteristics of a population hit by the different forms of poverty, from economic, material, cultural and psychological factors to the lack of possible and desirable futures".[1]

Starting in 1990, groups of urban guerillas began to be present in the neighborhoods of Comuna 13. Urban structures of the "National Liberation Army", ELN, with the Carlos Alirio Buitrago group, who called themselves "The Regionals" – the Luis Fernando Giraldo Builes group, and small groups of the Maria Cano, Heroes de Anori and Bernardo Lopez Arroyave, operated in the area. The urban guerillas of the "Revolutionary Armed Forces of Colombia," FARC, represented by the Teofilo Forero and rebels of the Jacobo Arenas groups also made their presence felt in the area.

On February 25th, 1996 the "People's Armed Commandos", CAP a self-appointed group of independent guerillas

---

[1]   Conflict and Socioeconomic Diagnosis of Comuna 13 Report. Government of Medellín. October 2002, p. 11

supported by the ELN rebels, was founded in Comuna 13. Before adopting its name, the CAP called themselves CAB; the Neighborhood Armed Commandos. Initially they were present in the neighborhoods of Juan XXIII, La Quiebra, Blanquizal, El Salado and later in other neighborhoods of the area.

Upon their arrival, the urban guerillas killed many members of other gangs who had taken position in the area before them and thus expelled them from the area. They installed their armed regime and largely exercised dominion over the Comuna by subduing the population, controlling all matters related to security, movement, and even communal living. The community had to go to the illegal groups to solve their problems. Otherwise, if they decided to talk to the legally constituted authorities, they could be subject to retaliation.

Each armed group had its own territories or neighborhoods where they exerted control and where other guerilla groups did not interfere. Over the years and with the increase in the number of members in these groups, disputes and armed clashes over territorial control began, which prompted the restriction of passage from one neighborhood to another. For example, the inhabitants of an area controlled by the ELN rebels could not pass through the neighborhoods controlled by the FARC guerillas or vice versa. The same thing happened with the CAP guerillas. Although these situations occurred only from time to time, they caused many deaths of members of the former armed groups and the civilian population.

At the beginning of the year 2000 the following paramilitary groups began to show up in Comuna 13: The José Luis Zuluaga group of the Peasants' self-defense of Magdalena Medio region ACMM, the Metro and Cacique Nutibara groups. This way, the worst armed conflict ever to take place in a Colombian city got started, concentrating guerilla, paramilitary groups and government forces.

The paramilitaries began their dispute with the FARC, ELN and CAP over territorial control, trying to banish them from the area. They began to execute armed operations against them and civilians, in San Javier-La Loma, Antonio Nariño, El Socorro, Belencito, Eduardo Santos, Betania y El Corazon neighborhoods, while recruiting residents of these sectors. Usually, deserters from the guerillas or those who had suffered some type of abuse at their hands. This took place in an environment "... where people's ideologies do not really matter, because the reality is that these groups took part in the conflict for economic profit, which led them to participate in exchange relations, or wage remuneration for services such as surveillance, area control or other things related to war"[2]

Urban guerilla groups got together to fight against the paramilitary and attack the security forces which had intervened in the area. "... Neighborhoods like El Salado, Las Independencias, Belencito, El Corazon and San Javier-La Loma, provided a backdrop for 'the urban conflict laboratory' as it was called by the civilian and military authorities of the city".[3]

For the armed groups established there, this sector of the city was the perfect place to commit many crimes with complete impunity. It also served as a refuge for those who took part in such actions and those who the authorities were looking for.

---

[2] Franco, Vilma, Liliana and Hernando Roldan Salas. "Urban conflict in Comuna 13 of Medellín City", Empresas Públicas de Medellín, 2003.

[3] Video: "Consolidation process of Comuna 13". Valle de Aburra Metropolitan Police. Script and narration: Nicolas Arismendi, December, 2002.

Kidnapping

As a result of the scourge of kidnapping in Medellín, many people's freedom had been violated by the illegal armed groups such as the guerillas and paramilitary and even common criminals. According to the Center for Criminological Research of the Metropolitan Police, in 2002 there were 65 kidnapping cases in the city, 35 of which were in Comuna 13. Most of these abductions took place in the form of ransom kidnapping during the time these armed groups were exercising their territorial dominance and control there.

1. Kidnapping for ransom

During the time of the armed conflict in the Comuna 13, armed groups used kidnapping for ransom as one of the ways to financially support themselves. In addition, they extorted wealthy people in the city, usually entrepreneurs and business people, through phone calls or sending them leaflets with logos allusive to such armed organizations. They also used this method of kidnapping to get financial resources to supply their needed logistical material and even to supply the fighters who were in other sectors of the department such as the rural area.

Kidnappings were mainly executed by FARC, the ELN and the CAP members, and were especially focused on people who would drive their vehicles into some neighborhoods of Comuna 13 such as Santa Monica and Laureles as well as the surrounding areas. These groups even managed to kidnap people in other areas of the city, such as the El Poblado neighborhood and other municipalities within the metropolitan area of Medellín like Envigado.

Inside Comuna 13, the victims were easy prey for kidnappers, because these organizations controlled the place and had reinforcements readily available in case the police got too close. That is why kidnappings took place at any time of the day or night. These thugs would set up illegal check points on some roads or would spring up by surprise, pointing their guns at the vehicles. Outside Comuna 13 they were vulnerable, because they ran the risk of being captured by the police when trying to kidnap someone. Therefore they preferred to do it quickly, usually in the early morning hours before sunrise, because at that time roads were not too congested or crowded.

On their way to commit a kidnapping, they would get into vehicles in small groups with short range weapons and leave in search of their victim: anyone who drove by or was riding in an automobile, people who were on their way to work or school, also people who walked or rode bicycles to stay fit. After threatening the victim, they would force them to get into the vehicle. These vehicles were almost always ones they had stolen days before. Then they would quickly transfer the kidnap victim towards one of the neighborhoods of Comuna 13[4]. There they would lock them up in houses or basements of homes of families previously thrown out of the area, then they would ask for the victim's personal information and begin the telephone blackmail with the family, threatening to kill the victim if the family talked to someone or reported the situation to the police.

These armed groups made some of the families living in Comuna 13 feed and hide kidnapped individuals in their

---

[4] See the "Forced Displacement" section

homes by threatening them. These families, as well as the people who were being held for ransom, were guarded by the kidnappers to avoid having someone call the police.[5] "Sometimes they would ask how many people lived in the house. If they responded four, then they would say now there are five, because they had to feed the other one, and did not have any choice. The fifth one was the kidnap victim."[6]

Carolina and her kidnapping drama

Carolina is a woman who at the young age of 20 was kidnapped by FARC members on her way to the University of Medellín, where, at the time, she was studying business administration. This is how she describes her experience:

"On October 15th, 2002, around 5:30 in the morning, a neighbor picked me up in his car in order to attend class at 6:00. When we were passing by the Laureles neighborhood a taxi cut us off. Inside the taxi there were three men. Two of them who were carrying short range weapons forced me to get out of the car and compelled me to get into the taxi. The guy who was with me could not do anything to prevent my kidnapping. Terrified by the situation, I told them: No, please let me out, let me go! One of the men responded: 'Take it easy, we're not going to rape you or rob you, the only thing we need is to know who you are'. I continued pleading with them to let me go, without them paying much attention.

Minutes later, around 6:00 in the morning, we arrived at the Veinte de Julio neighborhood in Comuna 13. The scene was

---

[5]   Source: Data department of "Sijin" section of National Police and the Executive Report of the Recuperation Process of Comuna 13. Criminology Investigations Center of the Valle de Aburrá Metropolitan Police, September 17th, 2003.

[6]   Domínguez, Edgar. "Forced Kidnappers". In: El Tiempo, October 24th, 2002, p. 6.

not pleasant, fear was evident all over the streets and the presence of armed people wandering everywhere was very clear. I was thinking "Oh my God, I am going to have to go through this", because I already knew that Comuna 13 had become a place of violence where people were killed every day. They took me out of the vehicle in an area where there were two men, with whom they met and spoke, as they kept me apart watching me. Afterwards I was left with one guy and the other one departed in the taxi. The person told me to climb the stairs up through a really steep area, which belongs to Veinte de Julio neighborhood.

'What is this, where am I going and why me?' It was the only thing running through my mind. At that moment, desperation was overwhelming me because I never thought that someday I would be kidnapped.

After moving up many steps amidst narrow alleyways, that person took me to a small room in which the stench of dead rat was sickening. It was very cold because there were other houses around which prevented sunlight from reaching this area. There were rats all over the place. There was a table and a rustic stove in the place that the kidnappers had set apart to keep me. Strangely enough, I never used to wear large jackets or sneakers, or take anything to eat to the university, but that day I did, as if because of some type of feminine intuition, I had gotten ready for what was to come. I thought many things and although I would tell myself to calm down, there were times when I would lose my calm and begin to tear at my hair. It is something you cannot control. In a situation like that, the only hope is your spiritual strength and your faith in God which empowers you to continue even in the middle of adversity.

After a few minutes, some men with their faces covered with ski masks began to show up. They came into the room for a moment without speaking and then stepped out, watching me the whole time from outside.

'Why me'? I asked the man who was watching me. He was the same guy who minutes earlier had brought me to this place. He told me to relax, that they had to find out who my family were. He told me not to be afraid, that war was very hard and I must not become sensitive or scared about anything. I answered him: "How can you say that, if the one who is being held captive is me", then he told me that people come into this world alone and when the time comes that is how we had to leave, alone, so that is how we had to live, alone. I asked him why he thought about life in such a cold manner and that I wanted to show him different things, to which he answered: "You do not have anything to teach me; the thing is that rich people have no idea how we poor people live; but it is good that they get to know how we live too".

I discovered that trying to understand a bandit's psychology or their way of thinking is very hard, because you do not know if they are telling the truth or just trying to confuse you. However, I would tell him what I thought, and he, sometimes, would give me his opinion and other times would just keep quiet. His intimidating look made me upset. On top of the things he would tell me and the anger I felt for being held against my will, the fact that he was watching me all the time, so I was not able to leave, run or scream, made me feel desperate. I kept asking myself: "My God, what are they going to do with me? Are they going to kill me or let me go?" I was afraid because I did not know what they were going to do with me. I thought that they could probably kill me and throw my body anywhere; then I asked that man to bring me some cigarettes and he brought me a whole box; so I spent the whole time smoking to try to calm my nerves.

At ten in the morning, two more people came into the room with their faces covered with ski masks. Initially, I noticed that one of them was a woman, because of the shape of her body. Once again I was filled with desperation, I started to pull my hair and cry inconsolably, while yelling out loud that I was going to die. I told them that if they did not let me go, I was going to kill myself. They understood my despair. After calming down a bit I told them to let me speak with my mother because I was okay but my family was worried without knowing what had happened to me and that made me sad. They laid a sheet on the cold floor so I could lie down. Minutes later they gave me some sugar water, an arepa [Slice made with mole corn] and scrambled eggs diced with onions and tomatoes for breakfast. I was disgusted, not because the food was simple, -sometimes you have to be humble-, but because it smelled horrible, and considering the situation I was in, food was the last thing on my mind. I did not feel like eating. The man with whom I had held a conversation with minutes earlier told me to eat, that I had to eat, he repeated that war was very hard and we did not know what could happen that night, that maybe we would have to go to another place where there would not be anything to eat. The things he told me made me even more doubtful. I used to cry a lot, I could see them staring at me: the girl came close and said to me: "No, don't cry, relax". And I responded: "How can you ask me to relax, this is not easy for me. Please let me go", I repeated insistently. However, because of the good treatment I received from the two that had recently come, who were a bit friendlier than the man that was watching me before, they were able to calm me down a little and got me to talk to them more freely. The day was passing by and all I wanted was to see the sun and leave. In order to pass the time and my desperation, those people invited me to play Parcheesi[7] and cards. Although their faces were covered with ski masks, their good treatment helped me not to be as scared as I was in the beginning.

At approximately two in the afternoon I felt very cold. I asked them to please take me outside for an instant in order to get some heat from the sun. They said no. I asked them to at least

---

[7] Popular board game.

let me see their faces, to allow me to see who I was speaking with, but they did not consent to that request either.

To pass the time, I started to write and draw in my notebooks. I made some drawings related to sadness, such as cloudy days, the rain and sad faces. I also drew star filled nights.

Later, at about four in the afternoon, the woman took off the ski mask that was covering her face. I was immediately surprised to see that the woman who was carrying a revolver and appeared to be dangerous, was only a teenager.

I asked her – "How old are you?"

"I am fifteen years old." - She responded.

"What!" - I said out loud.

"Yes, I am fifteen years old," - she said confirming her age. I was really surprised to see that she was only a young girl. Since she saw me writing a phrase on a small piece of paper, she asked me to show it to her; when I did, she told me to read it for her. I asked her:

"-What do you mean, you do not know how to read?"

-I am illiterate, I cannot read – she responded.

Her ignorance made me feel sad.

"-You make some really beautiful drawings, teach me how to draw –" she told me.

She told me a little about her life, telling me how she used to live in a farm because she was a coffee picker. She said that she always wanted to study but her parents never had the financial resources to pay for her education. Also, that she would constantly tell her father that she wanted to go to the town´s school to learn new things, but he used to tell her that he did not have any money to pay for school and that she had to work picking coffee in order to help pay for their basic needs. Her father had been killed by the paramilitary groups and from that moment on, hatred was born inside her.

"You know, what I feel is hate, you do not understand the resentment I feel in my heart", Leidy said, which was the name of this young girl. When I heard that, I felt a chill all over my body. When I asked her what else had happened in her life, she became mute as if her past had been so sad as for her not to want to tell me anything about it. I thought that anyhow, at that moment, I was with people who one way or another had to keep a barrier with me up, even if I was full of curiosity to know more about their past.

Later on, the man that came with Leidy also took off his ski mask. After a conversation, I found out that he was 28 years old and had joined the armed group at a very young age. I asked him: "What do you do in order to be able to kill?" He answered me that the first time he killed someone, he was not able to eat or sleep for days, and that he even dreamt about that person sometimes. That it was something very dramatic, but that it was hard getting home and not finding even a little bit to eat for himself and his family. Without anything to eat and no opportunities to provide for his family. Little by little he became an unfeeling person until reaching the point where nothing mattered to him and he would accept any offer in order to make money, even if he had to kill. He also told me that he did it out of need and not for pleasure. I asked him what he felt when taking someone's life and he told me that he did not care, because that is how he made a living.

The afternoon went by very slowly for me. When it was about 4:30 some shots were heard at distance. On the communication radio that Alexis had, which was the young man's name, there was a transmission coming through where someone was telling another person in a desperate tone to bring up the kid. I asked Alexis what that meant and he told me that the kid is code for a rifle. They used codes so that when the police intercepted their communication, they would not understand what they were talking about. Alexis also told me that they had seen a police patrol making rounds in the area from afar; so they had to shoot at them until they got them to leave.

At about five in the afternoon, suddenly someone knocked on the door and was calling out for someone to open it. Leidy went to open it; a moment later she returned and told me: "Our boss has arrived and needs to talk to you", and left the room with Alexis. I prayed quietly: "Dear God I put my trust in you"; I begged for divine protection. Suddenly, a fat man with his face covered by a ski mask entered the room. When he noticed I was praying, he asked me if I believed in God a lot. I said yes. Then he asked me why I was praying, and what was that good for, so I told him that it gave me strength. What else could I do if they had me against my will? I could not even look at his eyes, because he was wearing dark glasses. I felt angry for not even being able to stare into his eyes and about feeling defenseless in their hands because there was nothing I could do to regain my freedom.

In a very strong tone of voice, he asked me for my last name and if I had my identification documents with me. Precisely that day I had left my wallet at home where my documents were.

"Who are your parents, your uncles and what do they do? What does your family do?" – He asked me.

I was making up stuff not to put my family at risk in any way at the hands of these kidnappers; at the same time I told him that I wanted to know about my family. He told me that they had not been able to get in contact with them yet.

"But I have to know something, I am very worried" – I told him, and he responded that I could not know anything yet, to wait, that it was not possible. He asked me if I was taking any medications, so he could bring them to me. I asked him if they would keep me locked up for more time. I also worriedly screamed: "No, please! Why are you asking me all these things?" He told me not to worry, that when they found out what they needed to know about me, they would either let me go or negotiate my freedom with my family. Then he left and I stayed in the room with Alexis and Leidy, who continued watching me. I asked them if it was true that they would keep me locked up more time or let me go soon. Alexis told me to wait, to be patient, that maybe they would let me go, filling me with false hope. However, around sunset other men showed up at the room carrying a mattress and a big box full of provisions. When I saw them come in with that, I lost all hope of being released the same day. I asked one of them if I had to stay there that night and he said yes.

I yelled – "No, why are you going to do that to me, no please. I am going to die; I swear I am going to die."

He told me – "Let's hope things go well. Everything depends on what your family says; also, if there is no 'Rabble' [Referring to the police] in the area, it is easier for us to let you go."

In the evening they started preparing dinner. They gave me some fried potatoes which I ate even though I was not hungry at the time. But a few minutes later I threw up, from the tension and nervousness. I got to the point that whatever I ate, I would vomit.

Then I began to relax, I had to get used to it. In a way Alexis and Leidy treated me well, they would talk and play with me, and always took care of my needs. Somehow I started to feel a little affection for them, regardless of the circumstances and their cynicism. It is amazing how a person can be brainwashed like that.

As it became late, I started to think about how I would have to sleep inside that small and cold room and knowing that I was in an area where people were frequently murdered by groups of outlaws. I felt afraid that someone could come and hurt me. I asked Alexis about what was going to happen to me because I was very scared. He told me to relax, that the only thing that could happen was that they would take some of their positions, because they had trenches all over the area, and that they would have to move me to another place. When I heard that, I got even more worried. We continued playing Parcheesi and cards to take my mind off of things and not think about anything else that would worry me. Then, around midnight, I laid down on the mattress, without being able to sleep. I could see how Alexis and Leidy would nod off from time to time.

The night was apparently calm and it was silent. This silence was interrupted minutes later by bursts of gunfire, which in just a few minutes, interrupted the calmness in the area. That apparent calmness from minutes before turned into a nonstop shootout, and the streets were filled with crying and alarming screams. "They killed him, they killed our boy!" you could hear people saying. Outside, an all-out combat between the government forces and the armed illegal groups in the area was taking place. "But, my God what is this? This cannot be happening to me" I said to myself feeling very scared. The shooting was unbelievable, kids crying, dogs barking, cats meowing, people running from one place to another and the buzzing sound of bullets that crossed through the area could be heard. I asked Alexis and Leidy what was happening and asked them to take me out of there and to remove me to a safer place because I was going crazy. Alexis told me that we had to wait for the order to change places before doing anything. Time went by and the bullets did not stop, what was happening was horrible, constant bangs could be heard. Alexis' communication radio had ongoing transmissions. I heard voices that sounded frightened about the situation, communicating amongst themselves: "Son of a bitch, they got our weapons, they killed them, they found our stash, they got into Fulanito's house and caught him" they said under the tension. The shooting continued all night.

It was already eight in the morning when someone knocked hard on the door. "They came to kill me!" was the first thing that popped into my mind. When Leidy opened the door, a man entered and ordered her to take me out of that place, because they had taken over some of their positions. We immediately left the room, started going up some steps, walking while crouching and leaning on the walls of the houses along the way, so we would not be hit by the bullets which we felt pass near us and hit some of the houses in our path. One of my fears was that the government forces would not notice that I was a hostage and that they would mistake me for one of the bandits and shoot me because the people who were with me were wearing civilian clothing just as I was and there was no way to differentiate me from them. We continued on and we came up to a school on the high sector of the Las Independencias neighborhood. The guerilla members were entrenched there and I was able to see puddles of blood on the ground and red stains on the walls. There were people injured and a lot of screaming could be heard. I still remember the image of a woman with part of her face destroyed by the impact of a bullet. I was shocked to see such a cruel scene. I started to scream. My kidnappers took me into a house nearby where there were two corpses. One of them belonged to the man whom I had spoken with on the day before in the early moments of my kidnapping; the same man who had told me that we come into this world all alone and that was how we were supposed to leave it. That same man was lying on the floor with a bullet hole in his forehead. I started to scream again from fear. "Silence, silence, why are you screaming? Do you not see that we are desperate, can't you see that they have killed some of our comrades?" One of those men told me because I was making him more desperate with my screams. Suddenly, the fat man I had talked to before, their boss, came closer to us, not wearing the ski mask anymore, and said to

Leidy and Alexis: "You know what, take this girl downhill and get into the first house you can, but do not leave her here".

I walked with Alexis and Leidy down the steps in the middle of the shooting until we got to a house where there were several people. Amongst the chaos, they were not paying much attention anymore. I asked a lady that was there to please do me the favor of calling my house and letting my family know that I was okay. The lady told me that if she called, the police would arrive there and arrest everyone. However, later, the lady using signs and gestures, told me to write the telephone number down on a piece of paper, to take it to the last room in the house and leave it under the pillow. I wrote down the number and told Leidy to come lay down with me in the last room of the house. While we were there, I took out the piece of paper very carefully and placed it under the pillow, just as the lady had told me. A few minutes later a man came into the place where we were and told her to leave with me as soon as possible because the police were coming and were going door to door raiding each house and were a block away, so I was out of luck. We left there right away and ran through some alleyways and shrubs for a few minutes. I was really afraid of being shot. After a while, we got to the El Salado neighborhood. There I was taken into a house whose owner was forced to let us in. Later, Alexis left and I stayed with Leidy. I discreetly asked the owner of the house to please call my house, but he feared getting caught and then the group would get even by hurting him or his family, so he did not help me. I also asked him which way I could escape. He told me that I could take the stairs all the way down, but I never got the chance, because Leidy was always watching me. The hours went by and at about five in the afternoon Alexis came in with another man and told Leidy that they were taking me to another place. We left right away and walked until we got to another house in the same neighborhood where other men were gathered, among them the fat guy who commanded them. I asked him what he had found out about my family.

He responded by saying that my family had not wanted to negotiate my freedom yet but that they would release me, although not right away, because were they to let me go, things would get complicated for them because I could run to the Army or the Police and tell them where they had held me.

At six in the afternoon, they all dispersed and once again I left with the company of Alexis and Leidy to another place. We walked until reaching a house which was uninhabited at the time because the owner had not been able to come into the neighborhood due to the fighting. There was a phone in the house which they immediately put away. There was also a television and a radio. At least, I would have some way to entertain myself.

In the early evening there was some gunfire, but from then on the time went by in complete calm. There was an unbelievable silence; there was no shooting, no screams, not even dogs barking. The night slowly passed and I was able to sleep a little.

At about eight in the morning on October 17th, Alexis went out and I was left in the house with Leidy. Suddenly, two police officers, without imagining that I was being held hostage in that house, climbed on the balcony to see who was inside. Then Leidy threatening me with her gun made me get under the bed. When they left, she told me that if the Police came in, I had to grab the mop and start to mop so as to make it all look normal, that she would do all the talking and say that I was mute in order for them not to ask me anything.

Approximately at eleven in the morning, Leidy began to feel worried and I asked her what was wrong. She said she was very uneasy because her boyfriend was a guerilla member just like her and she was worried about him. She also told me that sometimes she felt forced into this but she had to do what was ordered to survive. She said that she wanted to leave the guerilla. I felt quite scared because I did not know if she was telling me the truth or if she was just trying to confuse me or listen to my opinion. That is why I just told her to do what her conscience told her to do and stop letting her heart guide her life. So, I told her to call her boyfriend, because maybe he was dead and she did not know about his passing. While we were talking, Alexis came in and he said things were not good and spoke separately with Leidy. She begged him not to leave her alone with me. He told her he had to leave because there were eight warrants for his arrest and he had to abandon the area as quickly as possible because if the police came in it would be "balls to the walls".

After Alexis left, I convinced Leidy to call her boyfriend. She did, but hung up as soon as someone answered. Very determined, I asked her to let me call my house. I told her that if she did not let me call, when Alexis came back I would tell him she had called her boyfriend knowing that she could not make any calls. Leidy started thinking and told me that she would let me call but not my house, it had to be some other place. She also made things more complicated for me when she told me that I could not speak but only listen when they answered the telephone. I said ok and that I would call somewhere else. I called to my boyfriend's house and they answered. I started to make noise hoping they would hear me. Leidy snatched the phone from me:

"You know what! They are going to see us and end up killing us." – She said. "Let's take it easy".

"Leidy, please" – "I said to her. It's just to talk to my boyfriend and to let him know that I am ok, and nothing else". She did not want to listen. A while later, Leidy went to the bathroom and forgot to disconnect the telephone. "I will call, even if she kills me", was the only thought that crossed my mind at that moment. I got up and dialed my boyfriend's house again and his brother answered.

-"Andres, Andres, I am ok", I am ok- I told him quickly. He asked me where I was. Suddenly I felt a strong blow to my head.

-"What happened bitch? You want to die or what?" - Leidy told me with her revolver in her hand.

-"No, no, no" – I responded. I was only checking to see if this telephone had Caller ID.

"Do not grab that phone again or you will have a problem with me, you will be in real trouble". After that she did not want to talk anymore.

When we were watching the midday newscast, we felt a strong thump. All of a sudden they knocked down the door and there was a strong voice yelling: "We are the Gaula of Colombia, Who is Carolina?" The police officers who were there to rescue me were asking for me. I responded euphorically: "Yes, I am, I am". They said: "We have her, we have her!", and they gave me a bullet proof vest to put on and the Police Department's Anti-Kidnapping Force's cap to wear. They immediately grabbed Leidy and the owner of the house who was just getting home at that precise moment. They made them squat with their hands on their heads. Leidy kept saying: "No, no, I am not a guerilla member, I was just delivering some water that I was told to bring" and kept staring at me as if hoping that I would back up her story.

Then, in the middle of a strong rainstorm that started at that moment, they put me into an armored police tank, where they also put Leidy and the owner of the house. Leidy, staring into my eyes, told me: "You know that I am innocent, you know I was just delivering some water, you know I am not the one who was watching you, right? Go ahead, please tell the truth, and say that I was not watching you." I told the officers: "Please do not do anything to her, please do not do anything to her". Then one of the officers told me: "Do not defend her, because she is a member of the guerilla and as many times as she would have been sent to guard you, she would have done it", and moved me to a different place so I would not look at her. I remember clearly her last words from the last time I saw her. When she was being taken out of the police tank, I turned and looked at her. She told me: "You know what? You are going to triumph, God bless you" and they instantly took her away.

They took me in the police tank to a place known as the Red Room, where there were more police and army officers, who were very happy about my rescue. Then I received a phone call from the Minister of Defense, telling me how happy she was about my rescue and adding some words of support. Afterwards, they moved me to the aid center the government and aid groups had set up in the Belencito neighborhood, where I was given a medical checkup. Anxious to see my family, I kept asking where they were; an officer told me that I still could not see them because they were at the Police Station in Laureles neighborhood. I told the officer: "What do you mean; I want to see them now". Later my parents arrived, and they hurriedly approached, in tandem with a bunch of journalists who also showed up.

When I got home, my family welcomed me back with a party. But I had come back with a horrible fear, so intense that I did not even want to live in that house anymore. That evening I slept alongside my whole family and some friends, because I wanted to feel protected. During the three days that I was held deprived of my freedom I lost four kilos, because I used to vomit everything I ate due to my nervousness.

That horrible experience left me with psychological trauma. There have been many times when I am traveling in a vehicle and another vehicle or a motorcycle has gotten too close, that I have felt fear and thought that it was someone who had come to harm me. Little by little I have been getting over these fears.

As for Leidy, the only thing I had heard was that she was sent to a reformatory. I never heard anything about Alexis and I testified on behalf of the house owner who was arrested by the police when he got home, because they mistook him for one of the kidnappers, stating that he did not have anything to do with my kidnapping.

I learned a lot from the most tragic experiences in life, because my experience was of a completely different reality from any you probably know and I learned to appreciate what I have: freedom, family and friends. As a person who has experienced a kidnapping, as a victim, I want to send a message of hope to those who have family members in captivity. Above everything else, have a lot of faith and keep hoping that someday you will have the chance to reunite with that loved one who has been deprived of his freedom. Pray to God with all your heart and strength, ask him for the gift of seeing them alive and free again.

Express Kidnapping

Express kidnapping was an idea brought on by the guerilla groups in Comuna 13. The idea was to get quick cash by kidnapping and use the money to finance their armed conflict in the area. This form of kidnapping took place more frequently in the Veinte de Julio, Santa Monica and San Javier neighborhoods. Some of the victims were residents of the Nueva Andalucía, San Michel and Abedules residential complexes, which are located near the Health Center. This type of kidnapping was carried out by small groups – mostly composed of underage combatants - who carried short range weapons, such as revolvers or 9mm pistols, and who would wait on the main roadways until a vehicle would pass by, generally one with two or more people on board.

Then they would pull out their weapons and point at the passengers, making them stop the vehicle so they could get in and then take them to the higher parts of the area. There, after frisking and investigating them, asking for the most personal information, they would demand a certain amount of money for their release.[8] They would usually begin asking for ten million pesos [Equivalent to approximately $3.990 USD at the time]. But when the kidnapped victims would say that they did not have that amount of money, they would negotiate and bargain down the sum. In most cases it would go down to less than about two million pesos [Equivalent to approximately $799 USD at the time]. There were some cases where the person being held got to negotiate down to three hundred [Equivalent to approximately $119 USD at the time] or four hundred thousand pesos [Equivalent to approximately $159 USD at the time]. There were even some situations, where the victims did not possess any money and were residents of the same area, so they had to negotiate their freedom or that of their companions in exchange for valuable things, such as a television set or a stereo.

Depending on the number of people the kidnappers nabbed, they would let one or two of them leave the area for a period of time of less than three hours, to get the money and come back. Meanwhile, they would keep their companions, threatening to kill them if the others did not come back or called the police. In those cases where there was only one person in the vehicle, they would take all the person's documents and get his or her personal information and keep the vehicle. After threatening the victim, they would let the person go and would give that individual a certain amount of time to return with the amount of money they were asking for. If the person

8   Sources Consulted: Sijín area systems and Comuna 13 Recuperation Process Executive Report. Criminology Investigations Center Valle de Aburrá Metropolitan Police. Medellín, 17th September 2003.

decided not to come back or to call the police, the kidnappers would retaliate, because they already had all their personal information and knew how to find them. That is why many victims did not report these situations to the police, and came back with the amount of money the kidnappers demanded.

If someone disobeyed their order to stop, when these groups were trying to pull off one of these types of kidnappings, the assailants would immediately start shooting at the vehicle. That is what took place on June 10th, 2002, with Professor Jose Ignacio Rua Arango, director of the CEIPA's Business Consulting Center and his son Wilmar Augusto Rua Lopez, a Business Administration and Aviation student, who were killed inside their vehicle when travelling in the La Ye sector of the Veinte de Julio neighborhood.

Families affected by Express Kidnapping

Henry[*] is an employee of the government of Medellín, who along with his wife and daughter, was a victim of an express kidnapping. On October 3rd, 2002, while all three were traveling in a vehicle near the aid center in the San Javier neighborhood. This is his testimony:

"I was in the car with my wife and my six-year-old daughter; we were on our way to visit my mother in the San Javier neighborhood, at about noon. We were passing by the health center, when I slowed down a bit. A young man, who was pointing a gun at us, approached the vehicle on the passenger's side where my wife was. The young man told us to continue driving slowly for one block and then turn left. He told us not to try to escape because further down his partners were positioned and they could shoot us. He was walking behind us. We did what he ordered and when we got to the place he had indicated, he got into the vehicle with us, in the back

---

* Name changed to protect his identity.

seat, where my daughter was. He told me to drive on, that he would tell me which way to go. I told him that if he wanted the car, just take it but not to hurt us. However, he made me drive to an area in the Veinte de Julio neighborhood, where he forced us to get out of the car and wait on the sidewalk. Some other men who were armed with pistols and revolvers came up to where we were. One of them told us that they were not going to hurt us, but that we had to wait for another person with whom we would have to talk (possibly a guerilla leader). After waiting for half an hour in that place, they made us walk uphill until we got to another location, where they made us wait approximately twenty minutes. Then a couple of men wearing ski masks to hide their faces, and armed with rifles arrived. One of them started interrogating me. He asked me what I did and where I worked. I told him that I was only an employee. Then he told me that we were being kidnapped, that in order for him to release my wife and daughter, I had to bring him ten million pesos in a period of three hours. I told him that it was impossible for me to bring that amount of money, because I did not have it, that I was not rich and that if he wanted to he could keep the car, a 1993 Renault 9. He told me that what he needed was cash, He asked me to get him six million pesos [Equivalent to approximately $2.394 USD at the time] instead and to bring it to him in exchange for my wife and daughter's freedom. I insisted that I did not have any money. He told me to get him four million pesos [Equivalent to approximately $1.596 USD at the time], and when he saw that I kept saying that I did not have any money, he gave me as a last option, to get one million two hundred thousand pesos [Equivalent to approximately $478 USD at the time] in two hours, to which I responded, that I would do everything possible. They sent me in another vehicle accompanied by another person who watched me very carefully, leaving my wife and daughter behind while I brought back the money.

Accompanied by that man I went home, and I also went to see some friends, from whom I was able to get the amount of money that they had asked me for. Afterwards, with the money in our possession, we went back to the place where they were keeping my wife and daughter. Once there, I gave the money to the man with whom I had negotiated. He gave the order to let us go and to give me back the car".

Health care workers, victims of express kidnappings

Alicia*, a dental assistant, had worked for fifteen years in health centers in the northeast area, places like the Santa Cruz intermediate unit, the health center in Aranjuez and the health center in the Pablo VI neighborhood. She talks about what she went through on two occasions when she was detained in Comuna 13 under the express kidnapping method:

"On September 17th, 2002, I was transferred to the health center in the semi-rural area of San Javier-La Loma. It was something very traumatic because they transferred me at a time of much violence in Comuna 13. At home everyone got very angry, my family was furious with me because I accepted the transfer. Anyway, I thought that Metrosalud was a very large company and I should work wherever they sent me.

On September 17th, the day that marked my third month working at La Loma Health Center, I went out to run an errand downtown with the dentist. On our way downtown at about 9:30 in the morning we were driving past the Veinte de Julio neighborhood, when suddenly two men and a young woman stopped in front of the car pointing at us with revolvers. They made us stop and forced us to get out of the vehicle, then they checked the car and asked where we worked.

Afterwards they ordered us to get back in the car and they also got in with us. They told the dentist to drive to the El Salado neighborhood's church. There, two other men appeared and made us get out of the car and pushed us through an alley

---

* Name changed to protect her identity.

on one side of the church. That day I thought I was going to die, that they would probably kill us. We saw that we were amongst FARC members; I looked back to see a guy who was coming with us, and I entered into shock when I saw that he had a grenade in his hand. For a moment I had considered the possibility of being able to escape, but it was impossible, because they also had long range weapons. Those men made us sit on the edge of a sidewalk and took the car. Later another man came and told us:

-"Let`s see, are you the paramilitary people who are taking care of those people of La Loma? Do not you know that there`s only paramilitary people over there?" We told him that over there, any person that showed up was taken care of, and that we were neutral in the conflict.

-"We cannot say we are going to take care of one and not the other, because our mission is not like that. As a health care group, the mission is to take care of whoever shows up; we have to take care of each person no matter their condition; we have to do it properly and well."

He was wearing a pair of blue jeans and a black shirt with the picture of Che Guevara on it, so I said to him:

-"Look, if you go wearing those jeans or that shirt, how am I supposed to know who you are or what you do, I have to take care of you and do it well."

-"Well, do not take care of those paramilitary people"- he replied. After a short conversation he left. After that, two other men showed up to cross-examine us and asked us some personal information.

-"Ok, how are we going to fix this?" – Said one of them, hoping we would offer them money. But we did not make any offer.

-"Look guys"- I said. "Give us back the car, because we have to run an urgent errand downtown."

-"Yes, take it easy, we will give you back the car in a little bit" -he responded.

-"We work to be able to provide for our families" – we said. "Our mission is to work and take care of sick people."

- "The problem is that you guys are the government" – someone else said. "The government is against us and has money."

- "The government has money but we do not" – I replied. "We live off our salary." After a while they gave us back the car with a burned coil and let us go without any more demands. Since we were not able to start the car, we pushed it out of the area, until we were able to take it to a repair shop outside that zone. Then we let our bosses know what had happened.

In the kidnapping they did not ask for any money in exchange for our freedom; however it was still very difficult for me because the guerilla members were accusing us of being members of an armed criminal group. The paramilitary groups had taken up positions in San Javier, the La Loma sector. Since this is a highly populated area, that is where the health center was located, which is where we worked. After that, when leaving La Loma Health Center we tried to alter our route a little, hoping that by this means we could avoid being detained again. However, as health care workers we were always the victims of these illegal armed groups.

On October 3rd, 2002, the health center's doctor, the dentist, the nurse, the medical assistant, the hygienist and myself, were coming down from the La Loma sector and were on our way to a meeting scheduled for 2:30 in the afternoon, at the intermediate unit medical center of the San Javier neighborhood. When we were getting to the corner of the block where the intermediate unit was located, three teenagers of about 15 or 16 years of age came out of nowhere. One of them pulled out a gun and stepped in front of the car pointing it at us. The other two got behind the car and were yelling at us: "Back up, back up, this is a kidnapping!" The nurse took out her rosary. The only thing I said was: "For me, the only consolation I have, is knowing that my burial is already paid for and that my mother knows where I keep the funeral documents".

The guy who had pointed the gun at us in front of the car, made the hygienist get into the back of the car and got into the front with the doctor and the dentist. The other two were escorting us, walking along both sides of the car. They made us go into Veinte de Julio neighborhood. We got to a corner and got out of the car; at that moment a lot of shots were heard coming from one side of the mountain. The people who had detained us were saying that they were being shot at and would get behind us as if we were their human shields. We started to walk uphill through some narrow stairways. I was moving very fast, and one of them told my partners: "Tell the lady to stop there and not to go any further". When I stopped, I saw a couple with a young girl in an alleyway. They had also been kidnapped and a man wearing a ski mask was watching them. I got really scared when I saw that.

The doctor told one of the guys: "Hey, we are doctors from the Intermediate Health Center". The young man replied: "This is a kidnapping".

We were told to sit on the steps of one of the stairways and a few moments later another man showed up. He called the dentist and asked him who was the owner of the vehicle we were using and demanded that he bring back ten million pesos [Equivalent to approximately $3.990 USD at the time] in three hours in order to let us go. The dentist told him that we did not have that much money, so we could not pay any ransom. However, he was able to negotiate our freedom for two million pesos [Equivalent to approximately $798 USD at the time]. After they had reached an agreement, I spoke to the man to try and reduce the amount he was asking for, by telling him:

-"We are poor; we live off this job. Let us go for five hundred thousand pesos"- [Equivalent to approximately $199 USD at the time]. But he was dead set on it being two million pesos. He called the nurse to separate her from the group, but we told him to leave her with us, since we were going to give him the money.

-"Ok" – he said. "But he goes to get the money by himself" – referring to the dentist.

-"I'm going with him" – intervened the doctor.

-"No, he goes alone."

-"Look, kid" – I told him. "Let both of them go because it is easier for them to get the money. The women will stay here, and if they don't come back with the money, you can do whatever you want with us."

- "Hold on a moment" – he said.

He spoke on the radio with some commander, and was authorized to let the dentist and the doctor leave to get the money. While we were there waiting, a resident of the area came out from one of the houses and while passing near us said: "God help you out of this," and left.

In that place silence was the rule, nobody dared to say anything.

The waiting was getting long and I started getting very thirsty; I told one of those guys to please buy me a soda. He called someone on the phone and asked for it. A few minutes later a guy showed up with the soda. I offered some to my coworkers but they did not want any. They were very nervous and did not speak much. The young man who brought me the soda told them: "Drink, because it will be about five days before you get the chance to have anything else". That sounded to me as if we did not get the two million in half an hour, they would lock us up for five days. That really got me confused and I thought we would have to call our families in order for them to get the money together.

At about five in the afternoon, a lady who lived in the area and who was probably coming back from work came by. When she saw us detained and knowing that there was nothing she could do to help us, she went into her house, left the front door wide open and started playing religious music on her stereo, really loudly, so we were able to hear it. It was as if she wanted to send us a message of hope and let us and the kidnappers know what she could not personally say out of fear. A child came out of the house and one of the men who was watching us told him; "Get inside the house immediately!"

The afternoon passed by slowly. At 5:30 pm the doctor and the dentist came back with the money. The doctor told those men:

-"Ok, let those girls go."

-"Yes, yes right away", – replied one of them. Our coworkers gave the money to the kidnappers, but they still waited half an hour to set us free, because they counted the money a couple of times and checked our bags carefully.

-"Nothing has happened here"- one of them told us while we were on our way down the stairways. –"We did not do anything to you and don´t tell anyone anything."-

-"Yes" – I responded, "But this is the second kidnapping we have gone through."

-"You can continue coming through with no problem"- he said. And after this, we left the area.

Metrosalud gave a loan of four hundred thousand pesos to each one of us [Equivalent to approximately $159 USD at the time], so we could pay back the doctor and dentist. So finally, that is what each of us ended up paying for our freedom.

The health center was closed for twenty-one days, because it was not safe for us to continue doing this important work. We went back to work after the authorities carried out the military operation Orion in the whole area of Comuna 13. In those days, we were receiving psychological treatment, and going to security meetings with the Police Department's Gaula Group.

According to the Criminology Investigations Center of the Metropolitan Police Department, in 2002, there were 35 reported cases of people kidnapped in Comuna 13 or other sectors within the metropolitan area, but taken to be held hostage in that sector of the city. Out of the 35 reported cases, 21 people were rescued by the police and military Gaula Groups (specialized anti-kidnapping units). In the other 14 cases, some people paid the ransom, others were set free without demanding any ransom and some were murdered. Out of the 21 rescued, 15 were adults and 6 were minors.[9]

2. Simple Kidnapping

This method of kidnapping was usually used by armed groups against people who were not from the area but who were visiting or were suspected members of the government forces or informants for the other armed groups. After detaining the person, they would investigate where they came from and who they were, a process that could take hours or even days. If the victims of this method of kidnapping were members of government forces, generally after holding them hostage for an indefinite time, they would kill them. That is what happened to members of the police investigative units who were working in neighborhoods of Comuna

---

[9] Comuna 13 Recuperation Process Executive Report. Criminology Investigations Center Valle de Aburrá Metropolitan Police. Medellín, 17th September 2003.

13 and to residents of the area who were in the military forces while they were at home or visiting their families.

After investigating the people whom they had detained, if the kidnappers decided that they did not pose a risk or if they did not have any money to pay a ransom, they would usually just let them go. They also kidnapped residents of the comuna, who were accused of being members of another armed group or of sympathizing with them, or being informants for the government forces. In some of these situations, after holding the victims hostage for a certain period of time and torturing them in horrible ways, they would murder them. This happened to two students from the "Future Creators" School in the El Corazon neighborhood, who were taken out of this educational institution by force on April 10th, 2002, and found dead the next day. (See the Infringed Childhood and Adolescence chapter).

When it came to government officials who were not part of the police or armed forces who were freed shortly after being detained, these armed groups would usually send messages and warnings to the authorities with them and other government employees, so that the authorities would keep out of the area and not take certain actions. Furthermore, they would indicate what the proper treatment which people incarcerated for the crime of rebellion should receive in jail was.

Juan Carlos* is an INPEC inspector (the National Penitentiaries and Jails Institute INPEC, the government institution in charge of the correctional system in Colombia) who narrates the story of his kidnapping. "On September 14th, 2002, at about 12 pm, I was ordered to get into a car belonging to the institution, on an official mission with four other INPEC guards. That day, near the Buen Pastor women's jail of Medellín, located in the

---

* Name changed to protect his identity.

jurisdiction of Comuna 13, we were caught unexpectedly, by approximately fifteen men who were carrying short and long range weapons (rifles, Uzi machine guns, mini Uzis and 9mm pistols). After being detained, they took the official weapons we were carrying (revolvers) and the vehicle, a Mazda 360 truck. They were constantly using foul language towards us and threatened to kill us. Later, some men wearing ski masks arrived in a taxi and made two of the guards get in the vehicle and took off with them. Then, an automobile with other men wearing ski masks to cover their faces as well, also arrived. They made the other two guards and me get into that vehicle to take us to the higher sector of Comuna 13.

They made us get out of the vehicle in an abandoned area. The other two guards were already there with the men who had made them get into the taxi. Then they made us lie down on the floor. They left me about thirty meters away from them, because I was the commander of the squad. The men with the ski masks kept saying they were going to kill us, as well as using foul language and cursing at us. When they were about to shoot the other guards, a fat man wearing a ski mask came down to where we all were. It seemed like he was their boss and he told them not to kill us. That person told one of them to return the vehicle to me, and this guy said he would bring it in a few minutes. Indeed, in about five minutes they gave us back the vehicle. We got in and left.

When we had driven approximately seven or eight blocks we were intercepted by another group of people, who were also wearing ski masks and carrying rifles. We could tell that there were even a couple of women in this group, when they also stopped us. I told them we had already been detained before, that they had taken our weapons and their boss had given the order to let us leave the area, and if they wanted to check if it was true, they could call him up on their radio. One of them told me members of the FARC operated in the higher part and that members of the ELN operated in the area we were now in. So it did not matter what happened before. We were now being detained by them.

They made us get out of the vehicle and took it; they searched us, took some equipment we still had with us, such as plastic ties and gun holsters, and made us ascend a steep street. What made the greatest impression on me, was seeing how people in the area looked at us from their balconies, or outside their houses, but no one dared to say anything. People just watched us pass by with resignation. We went up several steps, about two blocks, and they took us to a kind of improvised dungeon measuring one or two square meters, located in one corner of a house. I could see that this place was where they kept kidnap victims because there were ropes and ties with which I suppose they tied the hands and feet of the people they detained.

At that moment, I thought they would murder us because they kept saying that they were going to kill us. That if the FARC members had spared us, we were not going to be so lucky with them, so we needed to be ready to die. Psychologically that fills a person with fear. They asked us for some personal details, like our names, home addresses, phone numbers, etc. They also asked us how many children we had and how long we had been working for the institution. They warned us that they would call to verify if the information we had given was true, and if it was not, we would be killed even faster. We were there for approximately an hour. Then, a man came in and took me out of the dungeon. He took me outside and told me he had spoken to my superiors, and that they would respect our lives, but we would have to behave ourselves well inside the jails, especially with those inmates who were there for crimes of rebellion. At that moment, another man who seemed a bit agitated came close. He was so nervous, that by mistake he pulled the trigger of his gun and shot at the floor. My coworkers who were in the dungeon, thought I had been killed. When I was taken back to the cell, they were all crying.

Most of these men were very agitated and nervous, which made the situation even worse. Watching them in that state of mind, it was obvious that they might shoot us at any moment.

The man I had just spoken to offered us a soda. He told us to relax and wait for their commander to talk to us. About half an hour later, a man wearing a ski mask showed up. He identifed himself as the ELN commander for the northwest zone, and told us not to fear for our lives, that they were not going to hurt us. He as well as the guy I had spoken with before, had information that the INPEC guards mistreated inmates in jails, especially those who were there for crimes of rebellion. He told us that he was letting us live as a humanitarian gesture, since we had not been involved in any confrontation with them. He said that they were not murderers and according to him, they saw the deaths of government officials as casualties of the conflict in their war against the Government.

After a conversation, which lasted approximately fifteen minutes, he justified his cause and his intention of continuing the struggle; he told me that even he had been in jail. In the middle of our talk, an agitated fellow wearing a ski mask came running to where we were with a gun in his hand. He told the man who was talking to me, that Betty was coming up. Later on, I learned that Betty was the way they referred to the police tanks. So the boss gave the order to let us go. He told us to take off our uniform tops and give them to their men, because on occasion they used a similar dark blue uniform, and our shirts could be useful for them.

I asked him where our vehicle was, because we needed it. He told me it was near a school. I could not see it and I asked another guy where the school was; he told me it was two blocks down. We were able to run down to the school and just like he said, it was there with the keys still in the ignition. We immediately got in and began our exit from the area. There was a lot of shooting. We could see men who were shooting while crouching down, leaning on trees, laying down on the curves in the streets and on top of roofs.

Further ahead we ran into one of the police department's tanks. The officers got out of the tank and wrote down some of our information. We were able to contact the penitentiary, told the director what had happened, that we were now with the police and that fortunately for us we were free and unhurt. We were detained for three hours, by two different subversive groups, on the same day. After this incident, some weeks later, I experienced some episodes of unexplained fear, where I felt I was being followed, which led me to undergo psychological treatment. Furthermore, I had to move out of my apartment, among other security measures taken to protect my family, since people who detained us in Comuna 13 had gotten my personal information, home address, phone number and other info".

Other Barbaric Acts

1. Tactics of Terrorism

The armed groups used different Tactics of Terrorism, such as bombing with low and medium strength explosive devices made by hand with gun powder and shrapnel. They used vehicles rigged with explosives ("car bombs"), usually C4, R1 or dynamite. They also used "corpse bombs", the corpses of people that had been murdered attached to grenades.

"Car Bombs"

In the area, members of armed groups rigged vehicles with explosives to pull off terrorist attacks inside and outside Comuna 13.

One of these car bomb attacks that was prevented in this sector of the city was supposed to have taken place on October 16th, 2002 in the El Salado neighborhood. That day, guerilla members parked a bus rigged with approximately 40 kilos of dynamite and shrapnel on the side of the road, to make it explode when a police or military patrol passed by. The anti-explosives unit of the Sijín (Investigation and Judicial Police Section) was able to deactivate it, preventing it from causing many casualties.[10]

---

[10] Sources Consulted: Sijín Area Systems and Comuna 13 Recuperation Process Executive Report. Criminology Investigations Center Valle de Aburrá Metropolitan Police. Medellín, 17th September 2003.

One of the cases of terrorism with car bombs outside Comuna 13 occurred in the early morning hours on October 17th, 2002, on the corner of the Carrera 46 and 57th Street: in front of the Mirrors Building, where a car bomb loaded with 40 kilos of dynamite exploded. In this attack there were not any human casualties, but the damage caused was valued at about twenty million pesos [Equivalent to approximately $7.980 USD at the time]. The suspected bomber was killed by the police nearby when he shot at two police officers, while trying to avoid being captured.

"Corpse Bombs"

In order to carry out this method of terrorism, the rebels would kill a random person, then would turn the body face down and place a fragmentation grenade under it, after carefully removing the safety pin and pressing the body against the fuse mechanism. This way, it would explode when the body was moved by the authorities who had to process the crime scene.

Armed groups used this method of terrorism on two occasions in Comuna 13. The first case occurred on April 30th, 2002, in the La Torre sector of the Belencito neighborhood, where Police Sergeant Lazaro Correa Rodriguez was injured. The second occurred in the afternoon on August 31st of the same year, in the area known as "La Gallera", in the high sector of the Nuevos Conquistadores neighborhood, near the Police Station's current location. In the second case, even though the grenade exploded and destroyed the corpse, no one was injured, because the body had been moved by some residents with a rope from far away as a preventive measure.

Sergeant Lazaro Correa Rodriguez of the Metropolitan Police dedicated many years of service to the police institution. He worked in the anti-narcotics and counter guerilla groups in the state of Antioquia, where he was also station commander in some municipalities. In 1996, he came to Medellín to work in reinforcements and support groups in the central area of the city, and in 2000 he was sent to the Metropolitan Police CORAM squad, (the CORAM is the Motorized Reinforcements and Support Command). His work consisted of fighting crime in the whole metropolitan area. He narrates the difficult situations experienced in the central west area of the city:

"In 2001, as a result of the assault on Comuna 13 by paramilitary groups and the FARC, ELN and CAP rebels, we had to constantly go up to the area to counter their actions and keep them from attacking the civilian population. Every time they saw us coming they would shoot at us, so we were forced to defend ourselves. It was a very frustrating situation, but the worst event that I experienced was the one that changed my life forever.

On April 30th, 2002, at approximately eight in the morning, I arrived at the La Torre sector of the Belencito neighborhood with eleven police officers. Since I was in charge of the group, I spread them out strategically for two blocks, so that if we were attacked, we could react without being caught off guard.

Two of the officers found an abandoned house with a corpse inside and they informed me immediately. When we asked some of the residents of the area, they told us that in the early morning hours they had heard some shots, but they were afraid to come out and look. I walked to where the corpse was and I suspected that it could be on top of some type of explosive artifact because of the position in which it was left, face down. To avoid risks, we got a rope. I tied one end to the corpse's right arm and the other end to an officer who was outside the house. We got out of the house to protect ourselves from a possible explosion. Once outside in a safe place, we pulled on the corpse. We felt it turn and waited a few minutes. As we saw that it had not exploded, I, still doubting, carefully, observed the position of the body from where I was located. At that exact moment it suddenly exploded, and pieces of it landed on me. I felt a considerable impact on my face, neck, arms and legs, caused by the bone fragments and shrapnel coming from the body. My chest and abdomen were protected by a bullet proof vest. I could not see anything because my left eye was injured and my body was covered with the corpse's blood. Immediately after the explosion we started getting shot at from different spots.

I was really hurt; however, I was able to call for backup through the radio. One of my partners helped me reach the main road, where I was picked up by a patrol car that arrived a few minutes later and took me to the Las Americas clinic. I lost a lot of blood, fainted and was in coma for five days. I spent twelve days in the hospital and three months in the recovery process. I lost part of the sight in my left eye; my face, throat, legs and arms were pretty badly damaged.

After the three months in recovery, I wore my uniform again but under indefinite partial work disability. Nowadays, I cannot work in the operations area of police activity but I have been working in other areas that do not require or demand a lot of physical activity to get the job done. I still maintain that spirit of service to the people and to the National Police. Right now, I feel scarred physically and psychologically but I have always been able to counteract any mental trauma that has come close to affecting me".

Low impact explosive devices

The armed groups caused many victims among the civilian population by using handmade explosive artifacts. One example is the case of Alexandra Alvarez Londoño, an 11-year-old girl from the Las Independencias neighborhood. Alexandra used to live with her mother and five siblings. She was a student at the Refugio del Niño School, located in the same area, and worked at night and on weekends with two of her siblings and a nephew, selling roses at the Carrera 70 and 33rd Street in the City of Medellín. Flor Maria, Alexandra's mother tells her story:

"My daughter was an example for her friends. Even though she worked, she would never miss school because one of her biggest goals in life was to become a doctor. For her, seeing sick and suffering children used to hurt her feelings. She wanted to have the chance to heal them some day".

But Alexandra's dreams and goals were cut short forever at about 7:00 am, on June 17th, 2002, when she left her house with her eight-year-old nephew Santiago, on her way to the store to buy groceries for breakfast.

Alexandra walked one block; Santiago had stayed behind about four meters. Suddenly, from the highest sector of the neighborhood someone threw a handmade explosive artifact which contained bolts, nuts and screws inside, to increase its destructive capability. The artifact exploded when it hit the floor, really close to Alexandra, and shot out all its destructive elements towards the fragile body of the girl, who did not even have the chance to understand what was going on. Santiago, who was a little further back, received few wounds. Alexandra was lying on the floor with wounds all over her body. She lost a lot of blood, although she made her last effort to stand up for an instant and scream out; "Mom, mom, they killed me!", before she fell back down in the throes of death. Her life was coming to an end.

Santiago got up from the floor and went to tell Mrs. Flor Maria that Alexandra was severely wounded: "My girl!" desperately screamed Ms. Flor and ran towards where her dying daughter was stretched out. When she arrived and saw her bleeding on the ground, she, crying, said to her, "My baby, what happened to you?" Alexandra, with great effort, answered, "Mom,

mom, they killed me". Mrs. Flor picked her up in her arms and was yelling and begging for help to try to take her to the hospital. One of the neighbors who heard her screams came out and when he saw what was happening, he grabbed the little girl in his arms and immediately headed down the steps towards the intermediate unit medical center at the San Javier neighborhood. Due to the seriousness of her wounds, she was taken by ambulance to the San Vicente de Paul hospital. But it was not enough, because before she reached the hospital the flame of her life had been extinguished.

Ironically, that's how a child's life ended. A child who had found in her heart one of the major reasons for human existence - Love. "I still feel you near me, my baby, because I cannot accept the fact that I lost you forever", said her mother through her tears.

2. Crimes against life

"In 2001, there were 317 murders inside Comuna 13. Between 1st of January and October 16th, 2002, at the start of the military operation Orion, there were already 437 murders registered in the area, highlighting an 80% increase in violent deaths. There were still three months left in the year, which shows an average of 20 cases per week until that moment. All of them were committed directly by subversive structures of illegal criminal groups, such as urban guerillas from the FARC, ELN, CAP and illegal paramilitary organizations. These groups had total control of the area. Therefore none of these cases can be attributed to organized crime or other common criminals".[11]

Some of the reasons illegal armed groups executed residents of the area included: suspecting them of being informants

---

[11] Comuna 13 Recuperation Process Executive Report. Criminology Investigations Center Valle de Aburrá Metropolitan Police. Medellín, 17th September, 2003.

for other enemy groups, accusing them of using narcotics or being thieves, talking to members of the police or military forces, saying something against their group, denying the use of a vehicle or refusing to pay extortions or being a member of the armed forces or police. They could also be executed if someone pointed them out for some apparent reason or for refusing to join one of the armed groups. Furthermore, if some member of an armed group liked a resident´s girlfriend, he would kill the resident of the area in order to force the girl to become his girlfriend. Every now and then, members of the armed groups would tell the residents "the reasons" why they murdered some people, in order to justify their actions to the community. After killing someone they would tell the residents of the area they killed that person because "they were thieves, junkies, rapists or snitches".

Whenever they would decide to kill someone who was from the higher sectors of the comuna, they would take that person down to the lower areas, where there were vehicles circulating. After murdering the victim, they would stop any car and make its occupants put the corpse in the trunk, to take him to another place where authorities could process the corpse; because detectives and other police were not welcomed in the comuna; if they had to go into the area to process a crime scene, they would be shot with long range rifles. In fact, on occasions corpses stayed on the streets for days in the comuna because the authorities could not come in to process the crime scene.

"A high percentage of the victims consisted of members of the illegal armed groups, members of the government security forces, such as police officers, soldiers, undercover agents, and investigators who were also killed in the course of the conflict".[12]

---

[12] "Widows and orphans bear the repercussions of the urban conflict" by Ospina Zapata, Gustavo. Appeared in El Colombiano newspaper, Peace and Human Rights section on May 3rd, 2002.

Even with all these crimes and the suffering caused to so many families, the growing level of tolerance of the excessive violence continued to be alarming: "The introduction of death as an element that is present in the life of a family also involves the inclusion of a traumatic component in their personal and social environment. However, although a traumatic event is supposed to be something unexpected, in our society it has become a fortuitous and common matter; therefore, people end up acting as if they did not feel anything, as if the situation did not affect them at all, as if it did not hurt. The familiarity with physical, psychological and moral death is what constitutes the traumatic experience (prolonged in time); it becomes chronic and manifests itself, at the same time as the limits of the capacity for destruction seem to have gotten lost, and it also seems that at the subjective level there are no limits to our capacity for tolerance either".[13]

---

[13] Document: "The effects of war in boys, girls and adolescents" by Psychologist Angela Quintero Lopez, a teacher at La Independencia educational institution, 2002.

Photograph: Manuel Saldarriaga, El Colombiano Newspaper.

3. Forced Disappearance

In the area, armed groups forcibly disappeared people, accusing them of belonging to the opposite armed group, having an affinity with it or even for just being related to one of its members. Many families live in anguish and uncertainty because they have not received any news from their relatives in a long time and they still hope they are alive somewhere. Others just long for any information that will let them know where their missing relatives are buried.

Leidy Johana Suaza Londoño, who lived in the Veinte de Julio neighborhood, disappeared on September 26th, 2002, at the age of 19 after leaving her house to meet with her daughter Laura´s father. Her family still hopes to see her again. Morelia, the young woman´s mother says:

"My granddaughter´s father said that Leidy never met with him. Since that day I have gone to many official organizations, trying to find out about her whereabouts, but no one has given me any information yet. I have even been present at the exhumation of bodies from some communal graves that have been found in the San Cristobal[2] District, but I have not been able to find her. It has been quite a few years now since her disappearance and I keep hoping to see her again. All this has been very difficult for my granddaughter because even though she was very young when her mother disappeared, she still remembers and asks about her frequently. But I do not know what to tell her".

Leidy´s sister, Andrea, says:

"That day, at about 5:30 in the afternoon, Leidy called me and asked me if I could take care of her daughter Laura for a little while, that she was not going to delay because she was just going to pick up some money, but she never returned. We have a lot of faith that she will come back, even when people tell us that it has been too long and that if she has not returned, it is because she is dead. We believe that for God nothing is impossible, and we will not believe she is dead until we see her body. Why should we bury her in our minds because of what people say? We are hopeful that soon we will get news about her, irrespective of whether she is alive or dead.

Even though, at that time, Laura was only two years old, she has never forgotten her mom. She has always had her in her mind and asks about her a lot. She asks for her Tati, -that's what she called Leidy Jhoana. She cries for everything and we understand her. We express our love to her very much, but we are not able to tell her where her mom is, because we do not know. We cannot tell her that she has disappeared, because she is too young to understand what that means and we cannot tell her she is dead, because we do not know for sure. The love we give her is never going to replace the one her mom could have given her. But she is ok, even though she has become very aggressive and cries a lot. Laura's father was assassinated on January 19th, 2003. We tell Laura that her dad is in heaven and she accepts that a bit easier because she never met him.

I do not wish for anyone's death; I leave all that to God. On the contrary, I ask the people who might have her, or who could have possibly hurt her, that while they are doing bad things to other people, to think that they also have families and that something similar could happen to them. I ask God to forgive them and help them reconsider their actions".

On Saturday November 9th, 2002, in a wooded area of San Javier-La Loma, a communal grave was found with the corpses of three murdered people. Subsequently on the 1st, 2nd and 8th of August, 2003, another three communal graves were also found, these with thirteen more corpses. That came to a total of 16 corpses. The bodies of some people who had been reported as missing from neighborhoods in Comuna 13 since 2002 were found at these sites. However, nowadays, there is no news about Leidy Johana's whereabouts and her family continues living in constant uncertainty.

A news report in El Colombiano newspaper states that "According to testimonies of residents of Comuna 13, most of the victims were people who lived in the community at the time and were forced out of their homes, and taken to an area called La Loma, which borders with San Cristobal*, by suspected members of the illegal paramilitary groups".[14]

4. Forced Displacement

On July 18th, 1997, the condition displaced was regulated in Colombia under law 387, in which it is stated that: "Any person who has been forced to migrate within the national territory, abandoning his or her residence or habitual commercial activities, is considered displaced because his or her life, physical integrity, safety or personal freedoms have been violated or directly threatened, most commonly as a result of one of the following situations:

- Internal armed conflict.

- Internal disturbances or tensions.

- Widespread violence.

- Massive Human Rights violations.

- War Crimes or other circumstances stemming from any of the previous situations that may alter or have already disturbed the peace".

---

* Village that belongs to the Municipality of Medellín, it borders with Comuna 13.

[14] El Colombiano, "The number of Corpses found in graves in San Cristobal is already 10". August 3rd, 2003, p. 3/A.

In Comuna 13 many families were forcefully displaced by illegal armed groups. Occasionally, these groups would also incinerate these families' houses. That is what happened on July 4th, 2002: Early in the morning, in the upper sector of El Salado, a paramilitary squadron showed up, killed six residents and forced 60 families, made up of about four hundred people, to flee the area. Then they burned down 9 houses (built of wood) and destroyed everything that was inside the other houses.

Damaris** is an old widow, mother of four children, two boys and two girls. She arrived in 1992, to the high sector of El Salado coming from El Bagre town, Antioquia. She set herself up in the highest part of the mountain, in a small hovel made out of boards that a friend sold to her, at a very low price that she paid for in monthly installments. She had to endure many hardships and extreme poverty in order to survive with her kids. They were some of the ones who were displaced that 4th of July:

"My kids go to school, but since I do not have a job, it has been very difficult for me to buy the things they need: school supplies, uniforms and shoes. We have endured being without any food to eat and many basic necessities. They have even had to go to school sometimes without eating anything at all because there was absolutely nothing to eat at home. I have had to go knocking on doors from house to house and to the stores in the area, begging for food in order to survive with my children. The school financed my children's tuition so I could pay it week by week, and people who know us, as well as the neighborhood priest have sometimes provided us with school supplies.

In addition to all the needs we have had, we also faced oppression from the armed groups in the area. That night we were sleeping,

---

** Name changed for security reasons.

when at about one in the morning we were woken up by the sound of many shots and the screams and moans of people. I looked out the window and saw many of my neighbors who

were running, carrying some of their stuff from their homes. Some armed men were burning down their houses. I immediately grabbed my kids and started running with nothing more than the clothes on our bodies. I fell down several times while I was running and I could hear the buzzing sound of bullets passing near us. After running for a while having covered quite a distance and still hearing shots being fired, my children and I, very scared, knocked on the door of a house. The lady that opened the door let us in just in time, right before a bullet hit the window of her house. Fortunately, no one was hurt. We stayed there until sunrise, but we were not able to sleep because of the fear from the sound of the shooting that could still be heard.

The next day with other families, we took refuge in the Las Independencias School. We slept there for a few nights, sleeping on the classroom floors. Afterwards, the local government paid for three months' rent for each family to live in the lower sector of the neighborhood and gave us fifty thousand pesos so we could buy food.

After living in the rented house for three months, we went back to the area we had been displaced from. My hovel had not been burned down, but they had knocked down part of it; they had cut up almost everything, the beds, mattresses, and clothes, everything that was there. But since we did not have any other place to go, we had to settle into our hovel again.

We clearly still have the same needs. On occasions, when it rains, the water comes into the hovel dragging in lots of mud. I have not left because I have nowhere to go; if that was not the case, I would have done it. I hope someday someone helps me by giving me the opportunity to work, so that we can triumph over the sad reality that holds us down".

Some families decided to abandon their homes because they could not deal with the worsening of the armed conflict or to be exposed to it on a daily basis. That is why they chose to leave their houses at the disposition of the groups involved in the armed conflict and move to other areas of the city.

According to General Mario Montoya Uribe, "There is something that is very evident: people prefer to abandon their houses than to live under the dictatorship of these armed groups and to have to give them their children too".[15]

Many of the vacant houses that people left behind were used by the armed groups to live in and hide kidnap victims, guns or explosives. Others were sold or demolished. That is what happened to Angela's home, an elderly woman who, due to the fact that many bullets had already pierced the walls of her house, went to live at one of her daughters' house in the La Milagrosa neighborhood, on the east side of Medellín. A few days after being at that place, she was told by her other daughter, who still lived in the Nuevos Conquistadores neighborhood, that her house had been demolished using explosives, just as some other homes in the area had also been destoyed.

---

[15] General Mario Montoya Uribe. "Urban warfare hasn't prospered", in: El Colombiano. Medellín, May 2nd, 2002.

Photograph: Jaime Pérez, El Colombiano Newspaper.

Damaged Childhood and Adolescence

"As a consequence of the armed conflict, children's normal susceptibility is even worse. This susceptibility tends to get worse every time there are situations that directly affect social systems and the people who are involved in their care. Digging into the precariousness of personal existence, war is devastating for childhood and adolescence because it has, among others, the following effects: disintegration of families, and dismantling of social support networks. It also creates an atmosphere of distrust towards others, which in turn empowers attitudes and behaviors such as belligerence and confrontation and increases the sense of fear".[16]

In Comuna 13 many minors were victims of violent situations such as physical aggressions, rapes, forced recruitment into the illegal armed groups and forced displacement. In fact, "close to 230 children are amongst the group of 427 people that was forced to abandon their homes in the high sector of the El Salado neighborhood of Medellín by paramilitary groups.[17]

Furthermore, many minors were murdered by the armed groups in the conflict. Ricardo,* a resident in the Veinte de Julio neighborhood, relates:

---

[16] Document: "The effects of war on boys, girls and teenagers". Psychologist Angela Quintero Lopez, teacher at La Independencia Educational Institution, 2002.

[17] Urrego, Luis. "Massive Exodus in El Salado", In: El Tiempo, July 4th, 2002, p. 1.

* Name changed to protect his identity.

"On one occasion, around 8:00pm, I was on the balcony of my house, when I saw three gunmen with their faces covered by ski masks, who were taking a teenager of approximately 14 years of age with his hands tied behind his back, up one of the main roads of the neighborhood. Later, they shot him many times in cold blood and, after killing him, they calmly left the place".

"Stray" Bullets

Some minors were shot by bullets, either while outside on the streets or even inside their houses, as happened to Joan Sebastian, a boy who lived with his family in the La Independencia sector and who at the age of five was wounded by a bullet while inside his residence on May 21st, 2002.

Since early in the morning, neither he nor his family were able to sleep because of the constant sound of shots that could be heard. At about 7:30 am, Joan Sebastian was in the kitchen, located on the third floor, when all of the sudden a bullet came through one of the walls and impacted him in his back. When coming through the wall, the bullet broke off some fragments of cement that also penetrated his skin. Immediately, Joan started to bleed a lot. His mother, who was very scared, grabbed him in her arms and took him to the hospital in the middle of the shooting. His condition was very serious because the bullet that had embedded in his back was from a rifle. Fortunately, it did not kill him, because when it first hit the wall it lost a bit of speed. The boy spent four months in recovery and even though the doctors were able to extract the bullet, he still suffers from pain in his back due to some pieces of cement that the doctors were not able to take out.

Orphaned by armed conflict

The conflict in Comuna 13 left many kids without parents in the area. Some lost their father or their mother, but others lost both. That is what happened to Valentina, at the young age of four.

On October 5th, 2001, Valentina was at school near her house in the Veinte de Julio neighborhood with her kindergarten classmates. It was a calm morning and the kids were playing but suddenly that apparent calmness was interrupted by several shots outside. The kids got scared, some were crying, without knowing what was going on. Several of them saw from the school yard how some gunmen wearing ski masks murdered Valentina's father and ran inside where she was, to tell her what had happened. She was scared and did not understand what was going on, but she went outside to look. When she saw her dead father, laying on the floor in a puddle of blood, she was overwhelmed by tears. She was crying inconsolably, calling out for her father who was never again going to answer his young daughter's call because he had been forever silenced by criminals. The teacher, Catalina, picked Valentina up in her arms and took her to the living room, trying to calm her down a little. The girl suffered horrible trauma after seeing her father lying on the ground following the shooting.

The days went by and Valentina was very scared of sleeping alone and even of going to kindergarten. Her mother was her closest support and worked to supply her basic needs. But Valentina's pain would not end there, because destiny would once again forever put a mark on the girl's life, taking away the person she loved the most. Her mother was murdered on July 22nd, 2002 in the area known as La Ye in the Veinte de Julio neighborhood. When Valentina found out that her mother had been killed just as her father was she started crying inconsolably again, wondering why life was punishing her that way "Mommy, Mommy, do not leave me" she would say. Tears and fear had once again consumed her.

It has been a long time, and although her maternal and paternal grandmothers have taken care of her, giving her love and companionship, Valentina still suffers because of her parents' deaths. She seems sad and cries all the time. It has been very hard for her to see all the other kids with their parents, because she will never be with hers again.

Children stuck in crossfire

The children on the streets were frequently stuck in crossfire between the different sides. Many minors were almost hit by bullets and lived through moments of extreme anxiety after hearing the buzzing sound of bullets passing near them and striking against floor and walls.

Marlyes, a sports promoter and resident of the San Javier neighborhood, narrates what she and 25 kids had to live through in the area:

"On Saturday, March 9th, 2002, at about eight in the morning, I was next to the Nueva Andalucia residential complex in charge of 25 kids of ages ranging between 8 and 12 years old. We were waiting for the bus to pick us up and take us to the San Lorenzo soccer school in the municipality of Envigado. Suddenly, there was an armed confrontation and we were stuck in the middle of the shooting. We did not have any place to take shelter in, because the watchman of the residential complex closed the main gate and lay down on the floor as soon as the shooting started so that he would not get hit by the bullets. Also, all the houses that were nearby had their doors closed. We could feel the buzzing of the bullets passing near us. We were really scared and the kids were crying. We were screaming hysterically at the guard to open the gate for us because we were going to be killed. When he finally heard our screams, he immediately did open it for us. I took the children inside right away. I told them to lay down on the floor and not to lift their heads up and that nothing was going to happen to us because God was going to protect us. The shooting lasted about 20 minutes. The children were really frightened and could not stop crying. I kept trying to make them feel better and tried to calm them down a bit until the shooting stopped. A few minutes later when we could not hear any more shooting, the bus arrived. We got in it and went on our way to honour our commitment at the soccer school. The kids remained distracted the rest of the day".

Dream killer bullets

Yiseth Tascon Olarte lived in the Las Independencias neighborhood. At only eleven years old (On May 21st, 2002), she was at a payphone near her house with her mother, her sisters and her niece, calling the school to let them know that she would not be able to attend classes that day because there had been shootings going on in the area since early in the morning. While there, a shot was heard, and a bullet from a rifle struck Yiseth on the side and also wounded her niece Leidy who was 10 years old. Yiseth's mother, Maria Edilia Tascon, narrates:

"My little girl was very intelligent and affectionate; she used to study at the Las Independencias School, where she stood out for being a good student and classmate. Even if she woke up with fever, she would go to class because she did not like to miss school.

She used to love being next to me very much. She would tell me everything about herself, how she was doing in school. My dream was always to spend my future years next to her. In those days, she had recently told me that she was never going to let me be alone, that her wish for the future was to become a lawyer and that she was always going to be by my

79

side. But they killed her, along with my dreams. I think I will never be able to get over that. The night before her death, she had stayed up studying for a mathematics exam she had the next day until late at night. Since shooting could be heard from early in the morning, she was desperate because she wanted to go to school. I told her not to go, that maybe there were not any classes that day and she told me that she would call the school so she would not fail the math test. I told her that I would go with her to the payphone because there was no phone in our house. We went up the steps with my other daughters and a granddaughter on our way to the payphone; there were a lot of people, and the sound of bullets had ceased, so we were confident that the shooting had stopped; however, while we were there we heard a shot and I felt the buzzing of a bullet that passed near me. When I looked at Yiseth, I saw her wounded and bloodied: a shot had penetrated her side all the way through. I took her in my arms, she did not say anything, not even a groan, only an expression of disbelief on her face. My daughters took her out of my arms immediately to take her to the health center".

Leidy narrates:

"I felt something hot, a little burn, "*Ouch*!" I yelled. I saw that they were taking Yiseth away in the middle of a commotion. I said out loud: "I think I am wounded". Then a man who was nearby said that I was wounded, but I told him to be quiet, because I thought that they would turn their attention towards me instead of Yiseth, and she looked really bad. After they left with Yiseth towards the Aid Center, I went to Esperanza`s house, a lady who is well known in the neighborhood and I told her I was wounded. She looked at me and told some people to take me to the hospital because I was very pale. They took me to the San Javier`s health center and that is where I found out that Yiseth had passed away. I started crying. Then I was taken to another hospital in the city where they x-rayed me. I found out that I had a bullet inside of me and that they were not able to get it out. I was in the hospital for three months. I was very scared, because I did not want to go back to the neighborhood".

And Maria Edilia says:

"Yiseth`s death affected all of us a lot and we were overwhelmed by a very strong feeling of fear because the danger was still extremely real. I had already lived many years but it was not fair for the children and teenagers to have to live like that, full of fear. On top of being poor, they also lacked tranquility. I chose to leave the neighborhood to see if I could start over, but since I could not get over losing Yiseth, we came back six months later".

Lethal "Toys"

Many children were wounded by explosive devices after finding them abandoned on the streets and using them as their toys. That is what happened to some minors in the Nuevos Conquistadores neighborhood on March 29th, 2003, who were seriously wounded by a grenade round that exploded after they found it and started playing with it.

Faber, who at the time was nine years old, narrates the following: "I went out in the morning with my cousin Arturo to find recyclable aluminum material to sell. We were in the El Corazon neighborhood. When we were looking in a whole bunch of debris that was piled up there, we found something in the shape of a rocket, like the ones you see in the movies. Since it was dirty, we washed it and started playing with it next to a payphone where there were some other kids. I threw the rocket on the floor and picked it up several times. When I threw it pointing down hard against the floor, it exploded. At that moment I fell to the ground and the other children too. I was bleeding and started to scream. I had several wounds on my left hand and right foot.

Some people that were near, when they saw us wounded on the ground, picked us up and took us to the health center, where I was able to recover due to the fact that the wounds were not too serious".

Faber still has a piece of shrapnel embedded in his right ankle from what happened that day, because doctors could not remove it. But this was not the only experience that Faber ever had with an object of war. Months before, Faber and his friends had found some bullets. They lit up a bonfire and threw them in. After a few seconds of being exposed to the fire, the rounds exploded and one of the bullets grazed Faber's right hand. He still has the small scar that it left.

About what happened on that March 29th, Deisy Bibiana, who at that time was 14 years old, narrates the tragic experience which left her scarred forever:

"I was talking to a friend next to the payphone when I saw some kids playing with some object but I did not see what it was. Then suddenly I felt a strong explosion that shook the ground. I fell down and started bleeding at the same time. I could hear screams and the crying of other children which was mixing with mine because I was wounded really badly.

I had several pieces of shrapnel stuck in my abdomen, my left leg and my right hand, from which I had lost my index finger. I was stunned from the blast and hurting badly. Some people that were nearby put me in a taxi and sent me to the aid center where they decided to send me to the San Vicente hospital because of the seriousness of my wounds. I was in a fragile condition at the hospital for a month. Then I was taken back to my house, where I recovered as the months passed, and I improved my emotional state and health after a few months more. This event totally transformed my life".

Playing War

Some minors who lived in neighborhoods of Comuna 13 were forced to play a direct role and become part of the armed conflict. That's how, under threat, they took up arms and joined the conflicting armed groups. Others opted to abandon their homes and moved to other areas of the city.

Juan* is a young man from Comuna 13, who chose to abandon his house in the Nuevos Conquistadores neighborhood instead of joining one of the armed groups in the area: "I was threatened several times by the guerillas. They told me to join one of their groups because if I did not I would have to leave the neighborhood. I always refused their demands until in August, 2002, I was home with my mother and all of a sudden four gunmen entered. They made us lie down on the floor and told us that we had to leave the neighborhood because if we did not do it, they would kill us. All of this, just because I did not want to join their guerillas. After that I packed my things and went to live with an aunt. Most of the people I knew who joined these groups are all dead".

The following fragment of an official document shows the way in which some minors have been used by the different armed factions

"Some children, generally seven years old or older, were used by members of the illegal armed groups to carry guns, ammunition or explosives and to take and bring messages from one place to another. They were also used to gather information about the location or presence of the government forces and were even used to find out where certain residents of the neighborhood hung out, their behavior and who their friends were.

---

* Name changed to protect his identity.

Illustration: Camilo Cardona. De la Urbe Newspaper,
Issue No. 15, August 2002, page 10.

Minors were subjected to brain washing and radicalization by the illegal armed groups in order to forcibly involve them in the urban conflict. Some of them were trained as snipers, carrying rifles and long range weapons, and they also patrolled the area. Others were in charge of transporting and stashing the weapons, ammunition and explosives".[18]

The minors who were convinced to become an active part of these armed groups received training in war tactics, terrorist attacks and assassination techniques. Some of them were also entrusted with missions such as the murder of someone, in order to demonstrate whether they were useful to the organization or not.

This crude reality was experienced by children and teenagers, whom the conflicting groups manipulated in order to involve them in the conflict that took place in the area, thus changing their toys for weapons and their innocence for crime. This is the case of Andres[*], who while he was still a teenager living with his family in the El Salado neighborhood, was recruited by CAP rebels:

"I was 13 years old then, the oldest man in the house and the only one that worked. I worked washing cars and recycling so I could take some food to my family which was made up of my mother and three younger siblings. My father had abandoned us many years ago. One afternoon in October, in 1999, two young men who were members of the CAP rebels went to my house to propose that I join their armed group, promising they would pay me 50.000 pesos weekly [Equivalent to approximately $20 USD at the time], also food and clothes, so that I could help my family. At the chance of having the opportunity to provide for my family and to earn

---

[18] Comuna 13 Recuperation Process Executive Report. Criminology Investigations Center Valle de Aburrá Metropolitan Police. Medellín, 17th September, 2003.

[*] Name changed to protect his identity.

money, I did not think about the consequences of making that decision and I accepted. A few days later, they started teaching me and other teenagers between the ages of 11 and 16 years old everything to do with the organization's ideology, such as weapon and explosives handling. We learned to shoot several types of weapons, to fill bullets with cyanide and to kill a person in cold blood. They also taught us how to make low impact explosive devices and to introduce explosives in gas tanks. This training lasted five months. After that they ordered us to walk through some specific neighborhoods of Comuna 13, in order to find out who frequented the area. Initially, I was given a revolver. At night we would meet so we could tell each other which place we had to watch the next day. Fifteen days I kept following the same routine, when one of the guys that was in charge of us approached me and told me that I had to carry out the first execution to show what I was made of, otherwise I was not welcome in the group. The order was to kill a local guy who had been my friend since childhood because we lived on the same block. I did not want to kill him, there was no reason to. I thought about it a lot. However, because of the psychological pressure that I was under, I had to accept the order. The next day I was able to locate him and asked him to meet me at a certain time in a sector of the Veinte de Julio neighborhood to clear up a certain situation. Since that young man knew me, he did not suspect the real reason. I had asked him to meet me and arrive at our meeting on time. I showed up with another guy who had been in the guerillas longer than me. When I and the guy I had shown up with saw my friend, he took the first shot and hit him in the chest. Then I shot him twice. It was astonishing, the way I was becoming a cruel person since joining the armed group. Afterwards, I headed towards the commander who had entrusted the mission to me; I told him that I had already killed my friend and he congratulated me.

As time went by the conflict got worse, and I had to take part in confrontations against the authorities, I saw many people die. It was like that until October 18th, 2002, two days after the military operation Orion, when, after hiding for a while in my girlfriend's house, who was pregnant at the time, we were able to leave the area. My girlfriend hired a vehicle to transport our things. Then I hid inside a dresser that they loaded on the truck, so I could get out of the house and avoid being arrested by the police, who were all over the area. We went to another sector of the city where some family members offered to take us in. One of my cousins used to give me a lot of advice, he used to tell me to change, to turn myself in to the authorities, and little by little he convinced me. After being in that house for three months, I headed towards the ex-combatants reinsertion office located in the Alpujarra Government Center. There they started a process with me. They sent me to a battalion where I lived with soldiers for 40 days. They offered me their friendship and told me that I had made a good choice by getting out of the war to start over and begin a new life without guns. Then I was taken to the La Floresta Minors Protection Center, where they taught me how to make bracelets and necklaces for eight days. After that, they took me to Hogares Claret, a place where there were twelve more youngsters, between the ages of 10 and 17 years old, who had also been members of the guerilla or paramilitary groups. Our goal was to change, and that is why we avoided remembering our dark past. On the contrary, we shared, studied, played and became friends in no time. I was there for a few months and then I left because my family was in bad financial shape, and my girlfriend was about to give birth. I got a job washing cars in a parking lot, and with the money I earn, I have been able to help my family, doing honest work. Now, I hope to be able to provide for my family, and strive to be a good father. Joining an illegal armed group was total madness".

Some minors who were recruited by the illegal armed groups were taken out of the city and transferred to other sectors of the State of Antioquia where these groups had a strong presence. In those places, they were trained to become members of the rural guerilla or paramilitary groups. Once taken there, there was no turning back, they could not return to their former lives because they were then considered members of the groups in conflict and had to obey orders.

Carlos* is a young man who lived in the Los Nuevos Conquistadores neighborhood with his family, made up of his parents, two younger brothers and one younger sister, all minors. He narrates how he was recruited by the ELN, when he was still a teenager:

"In October, 2002, we were going through a rough financial situation, because my father was out of work. Since I was the oldest son in my family, at sixteen years old, I went out on several occasions to try to get a job, but because I was a minor, no one would hire me. One afternoon I was at home with my sister who was 15 years old then, when two men arrived offering us the opportunity to earn money. They invited us to join the ELN and assured us that they would pay us to work with them. They were able to convince us with their promises and warned us that we had to leave the city. But in December we would be allowed to come back home for a few weeks to bring money to our family. The next day, at four in the morning, my sister and I left the house and went to the Veinte de Julio neighborhood, where we were picked up in a bus. It took us to the rural area of the municipality of Alejandría, where we were turned in to the Bernardo Lopez Arroyave group of the ELN. We could not turn back and we had to accept their demands. One of them told us that we did not own ourselves anymore, that they were our family now. Then they took us to a camp in a dense wooded area. For the first three months we were subjected to rigorous physical training and received instructions on weapons and explosives handling.

After the first three months of training, they separated me from my sister and took me to another camp which was made

---

* Name changed to protect his identity.

up of minors; the youngest was 12 years old. Just like me, they had all been taken there with promises and lies.

Some months went by, and on June 17th, 2001, I met with my sister again. I went with her and five other guys to a little makeshift house which was abandoned, near a small village. At approximately twelve noon, while my sister was making something to eat in a wood burning stove and we were resting on top of some logs, a group of paramilitaries showed up at the house and opened fire on us. My sister was killed, as well as four of the other guys, because they did not have any time to react. When I went to grab my rifle, which I had left next to my feet, I was shot in the arm. Then I started running, I threw myself down a ravine and was able to escape, as did another one of the young men I was with.

After that incident, the commanders sent me to Medellín, where I spent two months recovering from the wound in my left arm. Once healed, they sent me to reinforce the ELN units in Comuna 13 where I lived. I took part in the armed confrontation in the area until on October 16th, 2002, when the government launched the military operation Orion, I was able to leave it. I went to the Santo Domingo neighborhood where I was active for one more month; but I was not with the ELN anymore I was already with the FARC guerillas. Finally, one day I invited two guys I trusted, who were also members of the FARC rebels, to escape from the organization with me. They accepted, and so we escaped to one of their houses. I was there for 15 days, then I went back home to my family, and avoided going out on the streets for several days. On December 19th, someone reported me to the police, so a few agents went to my house, patted me down and asked me for identification. Then they took me to the Sijin, where I spent several hours under investigation, and afterwards, because I was 17 years old, they took me to the reclusion center for minors in the La Floresta neighborhood, where I was held until the 31st of the same month. Then they took me to the Carlos Lleras Restrepo Center, also known as La Pola, in Medellín, from where I was set free on March 28th, 2003.

Now I live in Medellín City with my wife and son and I work in construction. Every day I ask God for a new opportunity to provide for my family, because due to my mistakes I lost many of my values and also my sister, whom I loved so much".

The conflict as experienced in the classrooms

Some classrooms were hit by the bullets, when the armed groups confronted each other in the neighborhoods of Comuna 13.

"It was not easy for them to concentrate in the classrooms, while listening, between fascination and fear, to the buzzing sound of the bullets, the bursts of rifle fire or explosions".[19]

In the most critical moments, teachers served as listeners, counselors and guides for students, motivating them to face the cruel reality they lived with on a daily basis. This is how it is described in an article by the El Colombiano newspaper: "The songs and clapping of children, accompanied by their teachers who tell them that the game consists of staying down on the floor, to minimize the sound of the combat that is going on a few meters away from the special school, near San Michel".[20] Maria Carolina Giraldo, a teacher at the San Vicente Ferrer School, remembers: "Frequently in class, I used to assign children as homework to draw how they perceived the neighborhood where they lived and they all coincided in representing it with warlike images, people laying on the floor or people with weapons. I felt the need to teach them values about the right to live and respect for others". This situation coincides with the affirmation in another journalistic article, according to which, "under these circumstances, the conflict

---

[19] Botero, Natalia. "Taken city", In: Semana Magazine, August 12th, 2002, p. 50.

[20] Restrepo, Carlos Olimpo. "Between Mariela Ibarguen and Luis Perez, death and fear". In: El Colombiano, Peace and Human Rights section, Medellín, May 31st, 2002.

Photograph: Donaldo Zuluaga, El Colombiano Newspaper.

of drawing dreams and fantasy characters, draw cemeteries, crosses and war landscapes".[21]

becomes a memory, almost a model for the kids, who instead Occasionally, in some schools, classes ended a few hours earlier than usual, so students and teachers could arrive home early. In other occasions, they found themselves trapped inside the school for several hours, after the normal school schedule, due to the bloody combats that were taking place in the area.

Maria del Carmen, who in 2002 was a fifth grade teacher at the Benedikta Zur-Nieden Educational Institution, in the San Javier headquarters, says: "Going to school to teach was often a difficult ordeal, because many times there was fierce combat in the area and the sound of shootings was heard all over. I remember that one day as I got off the bus near the school, I thought it was weird that the streets were empty and totally quiet. As I crossed, I found two corpses lying on the sidewalk by the school and they stayed there for most of the day.

I used to try to calm the children down when they showed up to class feeling scared, by telling them not to worry, that nothing bad would happen to them, that everything would be okay. I used to try to make them forget the violent scenes they often experienced in their neighborhoods, but most of the time we were not able to really concentrate well in class because children would be sharing among themselves what they had experienced in recent days like the finding of dead bodies lying on the ground or something that had happened to one of their family members or someone they knew. When the sound of shooting was heard, I used to guide the children to the corners of the classroom, where we would lie down on

---

[21] Ospina Zapata, Gustavo. "Widows and orphans carry the scars of the urban conflict", in: El Colombiano, Section Series, Medellín, May 3rd, 2002.

the floor until everything had ceased. But, on a few occasions, I noticed that some of them would grab objects, such as rulers or pencils, and would start playing as if they were gunmen, imitating what was going on near the school.

Children's parents who could not leave their houses out of fear of getting caught in the crossfire, used to call the school asking us to please keep the children inside and not let them leave alone, that they would pick them up as soon as they could.

After the conflict, students as well as teachers received psychological guidance from the Department of Education. I did not feel like I had the capacity to help with the mental trauma that the conflict had left on the children, because I myself had been psychologically affected by it."

Additionally, Jenny, a student at the El Refugio del Niño school, states: "The violence affected me a lot. I remember that many times on my way to school, I ran into people wearing ski masks to cover their faces and carrying weapons. When there were fierce shootings, I had no choice but to take shelter in any house that had its door open. I did not go to school on many occasions out of fear of getting hit by a bullet. The situation was very dangerous even inside the school, because on occasions bullets struck inside the classrooms. One day I was in the schoolyard with a friend, when suddenly we heard the buzzing sound of a bullet that passed by us and hit close to where we were playing.

In class, the teacher would try to cheer us up, by telling us not to worry, that God was going to protect us, to lie down on the floor and to keep our heads down; and to stay home and not come to class the next day if there was still shooting going on so that nothing would happen to us.

There was no safe shelter, not even at home. One day a bullet came through the wall and hit my mother in the right leg, and my four-year-old sister Jennifer in the head. She miraculously survived. A few months later, my fourteen-year-old brother Jhon Edward was murdered in the La Independencia neighborhood."

Another boy, an eighth grade student at the Las Independencias School narrates: "One day, I was playing in the street when the shooting began. I started running towards a house but nobody opened the door for me, so I went into the basement of another house. There was a man there; he had a gun and could not let me leave because we would be shot, so I had to stay there for more than five hours".[22]

Danger into the classrooms

Even inside schools students becoming victims of violence caused by the conflict. An example of this happened when a squad of gunmen went into a classroom inside the "Future Creators" School in the El Corazon neighborhood, and kidnapped three ninth graders in front of all the students. Minutes later they let one of them go and killed the other two after torturing them.

Camilo[*], one of the students from that school, narrates what happened: "I and my family moved to Medellín City in January 2002, from a small village in the municipality of San Carlos. We settled in El Corazon neighborhood of Comuna 13 with the goal of finding new employment opportunities for my parents, so my brother and I would have a better chance to continue our schooling. We soon started noticing the constant outbreaks of violence in the area; our dreams of getting ahead were being overshadowed; so much, that I was occasionally forced to experience the actions of the violent groups.

On April 10th, 2002, I was fifteen years old and a ninth grade

---

[22] Document: "The effects of war on boys, girls and teenagers". Psychologist Angela Quintero Lopez, a teacher at Las Independencias Educational Institution, 2002.

[*] Name changed to protect his identity.

student at the "Future Creators School" in the El Corazon neighborhood. It was six in the morning and my classmates and I had just gotten to class and were waiting for the technology teacher to arrive and begin the class. When she arrived, she did not notice that three gunmen came in behind her. These people had made the school doorman open the gate by threatening him. They came to the classroom where I was; one of the men stayed by the door and the other two came in. One of them said out loud, 'Whoever moves, you know what is going to happen. All men stand up.' But none of the students got up, because we were all so scared. When they saw that no one was getting up, they started scrutinizing each student as if looking for someone in particular. One of them looked at me and told me to get out of the classroom and after that two other classmates, 16 and 17 years old, were brought out as well. Outside, they started frisking us. They pointed their weapons at us and made us follow them. When we were passing through the main gate of the school, my uncle, who was the doorman at that time, was there. I told him, 'Uncle, what is going to happen to me?' He tried to approach me, but one of them pointed his gun at him and told him to stay still. He felt powerless because he was not able to do anything for us. At the entrance of the school there was a man, also armed, providing security for them. There was another one about half a block away, in front of the church, and two more further down. One of them asked the other if we were the snitches. He responded, 'yes they are', so we continued walking, escorted by six men, who were all armed. I was really frightened, you cannot imagine how much. I was praying every prayer I knew. I asked one of those men, what was their problem with me, and I told him that I was new in the neighborhood. Even though I kept asking the same question, he did not answer. However, after seeing my persistence, he asked one of the other two students that were with me what my name was. When he answered that my name was Camilo Zapata* that man was surprised, he put his hand on top of his

---

* Name changed to protect his identity.

head and told the other men, 'Oh shit guys, we got the wrong dude', and asked for my identification documents. I took out my identity card and showed it to him. He asked me to read it to him, and I told him it said my name. Then he pulled it away from my hand and took me to where the bus terminal was. There were about twenty more heavily armed gunmen there. That man went to show my identity card to one of the men who were there. Meanwhile, my two classmates were taken to a narrow alleyway near there.

After a few minutes, the person who had my identification card came towards me, gave it back and told me, 'Leave, and you saw nothing'. I feared I would be murdered from behind as soon as I took a couple of steps, but when I realized that they were really letting me go, I started running from that place. I came down the same way I had passed minutes before and headed towards the school. When I got there, a gunfight began in the area. My uncle opened the gate immediately so I could get inside and threw himself on me with a big hug, then went and alerted the teachers that I had made it back and was ok. I headed towards the classroom; when my classmates saw me, they all hugged me and were happy to see that I was ok. They were hugging me and asking me about what had happened. Then three teachers came and asked me to follow them to the assembly room. We were all really nervous there. They gave me some tea and asked me the whereabouts of the other two students. While I was telling them what had happened, some students who were family members and friends of the other two students who were still being held, came into the room. Because of the shooting they had heard, they imagined that they had already been killed. They were crying and the sister of one of them fainted.

My mother and brother showed up afterwards, as well as the mother of one of the other two students, who fainted when she found out what had happened. My mother, crying, asked one of the teachers if she could take me home. He told her, not yet, to wait a moment, because those guys were possibly still nearby. We waited a few hours inside the school and then at 10:30 in the morning, the teachers started calling the students' homes so that their guardians could pick them up. I headed home in the company of my mother and brother.

I found out later, that on the same day, at 11:30 in the morning, a man had called the school saying that one of the students was going to be freed. They needed his mother to go to the bus terminal accompanied by a teacher. She immediately headed to the place along with the school psychologist. They waited there for a few hours but the men never showed up with him".

A few days passed, then the two students' dead bodies were found in the Cuatro Esquinas sector of the Los Nuevos Conquistadores and in the Veinte de Julio neighborhoods. Their bodies showed signs of torture. The funeral was held the following day.

***

A ninth grade student from the Las Independencias Educational Institution comments: "I found out that weapons cause harm, destroy dreams. I do not wish anyone to have to live through the type of war we had to experience, because I know they will see death on every corner. The armed groups do not care what the community thinks, where you feel that life can end at any moment".[23]

Ms. Luz Nasly Garcia, a teacher at the Eduardo Santos School, relates her experience teaching in the middle of the conflict: "Basically, as a teacher, my work was focused on the mission of serving as support to students inside the classroom, providing affection, understanding, and being a shoulder to cry on when they were scared. I used to hug and motivate them. I used to focus class activities so that students could express themselves and act out their fears, with the objective

23 Document: "The effects of war on boys, girls and teenagers". Psychologist Angela Quintero Lopez, a teacher at Las Independencias Educational Institution, 2002.

of making them feel calm inside the classroom. That way they could develop affection and trust.

Whenever we were in the classroom and shooting broke out in the area, we used to sit on the floor, start talking and telling stories. Sometimes I did some relaxation therapy but it was hard because shots were heard all the time. Furthermore, I had to overcome my own fears because I knew students would be able to stay and feel calm only if I kept a cool attitude. I was saddened by the fact that in order to protect themselves, students had to sleep under their beds. Many of my students had stopped coming to school because their houses had been burned down, others had to stay home alone because their mother had to go to work. Many students were absent from class out of fear of being struck by a bullet or because they had been threatened. It was a very critical situation. Also, the lack of food in their homes was well known. One day, a girl came close to me and told me that when her father was on his way home with the week´s groceries, he had been robbed and that is why they did not have anything to eat, so they were starving. Another boy told me that his father had gotten fired from his job because once he was not able to go to work due to the shootings. All these situations were part of the experiences students told me constantly. I used to share what I brought to eat with some of them. It really hurt me deeply, the fact that I felt powerless, not being able to do anything to help them. On many occasions, when they came to me for consolation, I did not hold back anymore and started crying alongside them. Even though it was very difficult to face the challenge of teaching them what they had to learn, and at the same time becoming part of their support system during the most difficult circumstances, it was an experience from which I learned a lot alongside those people that I love, my students".

A ninth grade student from the Las Independencias Educational Institution remembers: "Days and nights were always one and the same; we had to wake up, not with the singing of birds, but to the buzzing of the bullets that were coming from every direction. At the end of the day, the war had also finished with the lives of many innocent people".[24]

Mrs. Sonia Maria Bedoya, a teacher from the "Future Creators" School, talks about what teaching under those conditions meant to her:

"I started working at the institution on March 2002, teaching 42 students in fourth grade. It was my first work experience because I had recently graduated from college. The first day, when I got to class and greeted the students, the fact that they ignored my greetings as if I was not there made an impression on me. Regardless of what had happened, three students took off their t-shirts and covered their faces with them, they put their feet on the desks and pressured the other students into acting up also. I evaluated the group and tried to do some group dynamics with the students to get to know their names, but many resisted and showed an unpleasant attitude. As days passed I was very surprised to find kids with switchblades or smoking cigarettes in my classroom. It was a really tough environment. I was really discouraged that week, and the idea of quitting and not working in that sector of the city crossed my mind. But at the same time I realized that it was a challenge I had to face. Although it was emotionally tough to adapt to that situation, I started by looking into the lifestyle of the three students who showed the greatest resistance to the rules and other behavioral problems. I found out that a student's family had been displaced by the violence. That situation worried me a lot and I asked the parents to become involved in a process to increase sensitivity and understanding of values in the students. In that way, we were able to achieve a decrease in their levels of aggression and a growth in their interest in learning.

---

[24] Document: "The effects of war on boys, girls and teenagers". Psychologist Angela Quintero Lopez, a teacher at Las Independencias Educational Institution, 2002.

In general, I became interested in analyzing the problems of the students in my group, because several of them were very aggressive, showed symptoms of hyperactivity and it was difficult for them to concentrate on studying. But the problem came from home because in some of their homes there was domestic violence and sexual abuse. In other cases, students had to work after school doing any job that came up in order to help provide for their families. Another cause of the problem was the loss of loved ones due to the violence that had taken place over the area. One time, a kid came to tell me that he would probably not come back to school again because he was going to join an armed group; that he had the chance to make some money without having to study. I told him, 'Do not go; stay here, because that is the short path'. Then I drew two paths on the board. On one I wrote THE ROAD TO LONG LIFE, and on the other THE ROAD TO SHORT LIFE. I told him, 'Here you have these two options, you choose. If you want to live a long time, fight for your goals and live worry free, you can stay here in school. But if you want to choose the short path, you are the one who chooses. If you choose the short path you do not have to be here, but your life may disappear in one breath'. The time passed and that kid opted to stay in school. However, I was saddened by the fact that other students had left school to join some of the illegal armed groups.

Now, for most of the students, school became the second home, where they stayed after classes, and even play on the premises a lot of the time.

My message for teachers who find themselves in a similar situation to the one I had to face, is to never give up, and accept the challenge of trying to help those children and young people. They need us to guide them to the path they should choose in life because they are at an age where they experience new things and that is when we should show them the right way".

Youth Living through the Conflict

Manuel Lopez is a psychologist, graduated from Antioquia University. He has worked in clinical psychology, and drug dependency prevention processes for teenagers. He has also worked as a teacher for youth development in the YMCA (Young Men's Christian Association.) in the San Javier neighborhood. Lopez explains a little about the discrimination against teenagers from an area such as Comuna 13 of Medellín, at the time of the armed conflict:

"The sociopolitical conflict was experienced by people of all ages but the situation of the teenagers I think was quite particular because they lived with a stigma that became worse during that time. There is a cultural ambivalence, according to which young people are important, and we say that he or she is the future, that young people have all types of opportunities to be successful. But other times we say that young people are dangerous, that they do not do anything and they are lost. Sometimes they are the future, other times they are lazy. Society is always pointing that out. During the conflict, in most cases, young people were seen as dangerous because most of the groups equipped with weapons were made up of young people; this age group was the most involved in the conflict".

In Comuna 13, many young people joined illegal armed groups, some of them were convinced by promises of making money, others forced to join, and others joined in order to be able to carry guns and feel "powerful", some others to become popular among the neighborhood girls and also to protect themselves from other armed groups that wanted to harm them. "The young people from those neighborhoods had fallen once and again into the illusion of believing that the illegal armed groups would provide them with some importance and wellbeing".[25]

In this area, some young women were raped by members of the illegal armed groups, or forced to live with them. Johana, a resident of the area, remembers: "In my neighborhood there was an urban guerilla member who fell in love with a girl, and she did not pay any attention to him. Once, while he was drunk, he raped her and shot her in the leg."[26]

Patricia, the head nurse at the medical center of San Javier, narrates: "I remember that a very beautiful young girl showed up. She wanted to know how a woman could find out if she was pregnant, with the obvious excuse that she was getting the information for a friend and not for her. She finally confessed to me that two days before a member of the paramilitary group raped her. "Why did you let him?" I asked her. "How could I resist, if he put a gun to my head?" she answered".[27]

---

[25] Semana Magazine. "Fear in Comuna 13. Publication No. 1.150, May 16th 2004.

[26] Johana, in: Comuna 13: Chronicles of an urban war. 2nd Edition. Ricardo Aricapa. Universidad de Antioquia, Medellín, 2005, p. 124.

[27] Patricia, Head Nurse at San Javier intermediate unit. In: Comuna 13: Chronicles of an urban war. 2nd Edition. Ricardo Aricapa. Universidad de Antioquia, Medellín, 2005, p. 191.

Photograph: Donaldo Zuluaga, El Colombiano Newspaper.

Walking dangerous paths

When the situation became tense in the area because of the gun fights, many young people avoided leaving their homes, abandoning their school and work commitments in order to safeguard their lives. The ones who risked going out, occasionally had to deal with the consequences.

Ms. Bertha Ines Gomez, resident of the Veinte de Julio neighborhood, and a psychology student, narrates the dramatic situation she had to live through in her neighborhood around 4:00 pm on August 7th, 2002:

"That day, I was coming back from downtown by taxi; after it turned near the Nueva Andalucia residential complex heading towards the Veinte de Julio neighborhood, a fierce shootout broke out and a bullet struck the driver in the head, killing him instantly. However, his foot was stuck to the gas pedal pressing it down. The car kept going fast towards the end of the road, where there was a pile of sand. It passed over the sand and fell into a small creek. I was there for about 45 minutes without receiving any help. Nobody dared to help me. Then the area residents helped me get out of the car, which had gotten damaged pretty badly so the doors could not open. They had to tilt it to get me out. They immediately took me to the San Javier Medical Center, where I received first aid. Then I was transferred to the General Hospital, where I was diagnosed with a ruptured tendon in the right quadriceps, a fracture on the left first metacarpus, injury to the wing of the right nostril and a close fracture to the left femur. Ten days later I was discharged from the hospital, but I was under temporary disability for six months and undergoing treatment for fourteen months. About what happened, I could say that it was an accident that could happen to anyone in the middle of a war".

Lots of young people dared to be on the streets even in the middle of the prolonged shootouts that happened daily; even as bad as the conflict got, they did not stop going to school or work, in order to achieve their goals.

Mr. William, a young resident of the Nuevos Conquistadores neighborhood, who was finishing his Systems Engineering studies at Antioquia University, narrates the difficult moments experienced in his neighborhood on his way to the university:

"In 2002 when the conflict worsened, it was a bit difficult for me because I had to work more. That is why I became an artisan; I used to sell handicrafts from house to house and from town to town on weekends, trying to earn some money to pay my university expenses and not be another burden for my mother, who had tried to earn enough money to set up a small store here, in the neighborhood. After feeling tired from working so much in other people's homes.

When on my way to school, suddenly a shootout began, I was forced to hide behind any structure I found, so I would not get wounded or killed. Sometimes, I took different routes: if the bullets were heard on the east side, I used to go through the west side; I guess that is when I started getting a little bit used to the violence. Our neighborhood is a natural trench line and the mountains protected us. It is ironic anyway, because it was precisely that natural trench line that did not allow authorities to be able to nab the criminals. Many times, I tried to avoid the shooting by taking different routes each day. I used to ask the men on the roofs about which side the shootouts were taking place, so I could know which route to take. They pointed me the way and told me, 'Take that route because the other one is dangerous now'; 'go back home', or 'this is not a good time to leave'. There were some days when I was not even able to go to the university. On many occasions, even all the precautions I took were not enough. I would be trapped in the middle of the shootout, I would see the person next to me get shot or feel how the bullets hit the walls, the posts or the tree branches. If you hit the ground, you could also get shot, so you should not stop, you had to continue on and hope not to be hit; close your eyes, believe in God and think that, 'If he has a reason for me to be here then I am not going to die, this is not the day, it cannot be today'. Every night when I would go up to my house, I used to think someone was pointing a gun at me, it was stressful. I would not feel calm until I got inside my house, because even there I had to make sure I placed my bed in such a way as to not get hit by a bullet. I used to think that if I placed it behind the walls, the bullets could never reach me. Also, because my house was surrounded by four other houses, I used to think that before they would kill me, they had to kill many more. It is a bit embarrassing to say that when I would see someone else get killed, I used to feel glad, not because the person got killed, but because it had not been me. I feel ashamed to admit it, but it is true. I used to think that tomorrow would be another day, and maybe it would be my turn. I used to think that I was in the crosshairs, in the eye of the murderer, and just expected to be shot at any moment".

Some young people from the area, who were studying criminology or had manifested their desire to serve in the Army, were threatened by members of the illegal armed groups. This is Junior's testimony: "I am a resident of the Veinte de Julio neighborhood. When I was 15 years old, I started playing soccer with the youth leagues of Atletico Nacional professional soccer club and I had to quit because I was suffering from asthma. I wanted to do good things for my family, to help them get ahead. But my dreams were frustrated by some situations and circumstances in life, which I am now going to describe. I finished high school and got a scholarship to study criminology. I started doing that at the same time as the problems in Comuna began to get worse. One day I was with some of my friends in the neighborhood, when some guys from an illegal armed group called me over and told me that they knew what I was studying. They gave me an ultimatum, to either quit my studies on my own or they would make me quit, by making my family pay the consequences of my studies. They were many and they had the power, so I had to quit and accept it because my family was more important to me than what I was studying. At that time my career was very important to me, but they did not give me any other choice. I asked myself who may have told them about what I was studying, if supposedly the only people who knew that, were members of my family. Not even my friends knew what I was studying, but anyway, all of a sudden they found out and that was the end of my studies".

For young people who made a great effort to get ahead, and who with tenacity and dedication used to try to open a way for themselves through some form of art, such as music, their dreams were frustrated because they lacked the financial resources to cover their expenses. But that was not the only obstacle that they encountered: they used to be threatened by members of the illegal armed groups, who prohibited them from getting together when they wanted to rehearse in groups, because they thought that these young people were forming a gang. This way they extinguished the hope and achievements these young people had worked for. Mauricio* says: "I came to Medellín with my family in 1993. I am originally from the Department of Chocó. Initially we set ourselves up to live in the La Francia sector of the Andalucia neighborhood, but in 1995 we moved to the La Independencia II neighborhood of Comuna 13.

By the end of 1997, we had a cultural show at school, in which my friends and I had to sing and dance. We liked it a lot so we agreed on starting a rap music group, which we named *The Latin Flow*. We started writing and singing songs about social topics, basically singing about non-violence and the different social problems we experience in these neighborhoods. Our group had sixteen members and culture promoters, but, because of the way we dressed, many people saw us as drug addicts.

---

* Name changed to protect his identity.

Near the end of 1999, some masked gunmen went to each one of our homes. They made us go to the neighborhood soccer field and threatened to kill us, because according to them we were a gang. We were very scared and asked them why they wanted to kill us if all we were doing was singing and dancing. They said that they were going to give us a break, but we had to stop meeting as a group. However, we continued to rehearse in secret.

We stopped rehearsing for a few months in 2001 because of the violence that was taking place in the neighborhood. Some people who wanted to help us and who came from other neighborhoods were pointed out as informants, so their lives were in danger. In spite of all the problems, we performed in Bogota city, in the Municipality of Sonsón and here in Medellín, at the Metropolitan Theatre, at Alpujarra Government Center, at the Convention Center, and in some other neighborhoods of the city.

In 2002, some of the young men who made up the musical group felt persecuted by the illegal armed factions and opted to abandon the group. So, the group was formed with only four members. We decided to promote our own songs. My mother got a loan and with that money we bought a computer, which unfortunately started giving us problems. We took it to someone to get it fixed, but that person left the neighborhood with our computer, and there was no way to find him or to know of his whereabouts.

Nowadays, although we have recorded more than fifteen songs, some of them as Reggaeton and Hip Hop, we have been forced to suspend our endeavor for a while, due mainly to a lack of financial resources and support. Sadly, none of us have a job, and we do not get any support from public or private entities".

When bullets went beyond the limits of Comuna 13

Some young people from Comunas 7 and 12 also died in their homes or inside schools, after being reached by bullets that had crossed long distances from Comuna 13, where shootouts between the different armed factions were taking place. "That's what happened on Friday August 16th, when a bullet fired from a rifle killed Oscar Dario Tamayo Lorza, a Civil Engineering student".[28]

Laura Cecilia Betancur was a 20-year-old woman, who lived in the Santa Monica neighborhood of Comuna 12. She was in her sixth semester at Antioquia University studying to become a Public Accountant. On October 14th, 2002, a gunfire broke out in the Belencito neighborhood. At approximately 9:00 in the morning, Laura was in her bedroom with her friend Natalia; they met for the purpose of studying for their next midterm exam. That day fate was not her friend, because a bullet from a rifle round came through a small window in the bedroom and hit her in the chest, killing her instantly. When Natalia saw her friend lying on the floor, she was terrified and left the room to ask for help for her friend, but it was too late. Laura had died just because she lived in a neighborhood which bordered Comuna 13, where the urban conflict was taking place.

El Colombiano newspaper stated, "According to studies carried out by the ballistic laboratory of Medellín's Metropolitan Police, it is not unlikely for a bullet fired in one of the neighborhoods where there are firefights -those that most people think are very far from theirs- to travel many kilometers. They are using machine guns such as the M-60, which has a maximum effective range of 3,600 meters (more than 3 km), and AK-47 rifles, which have a maximum effective

---

[28] Yarce, Elizabeth. "Streets under fire", In: El Colombiano, Section: Peace and Human Rights, 25th of August 2002.

Photograph: Jaime Pérez, El Colombiano Newspaper.

range of 1,600 meters (1.5 km), explained one of the experts. These distances can vary depending on the wind currents, the weather and the place that it is fired from".[29]

Miguel Alejandro Quiroga Bustamante was a young man who, at the early age of 18, was in his fourth semester at EAFIT University. He was studying to become a systems engineer and lived in the Cristobal neighborhood of Comuna 12.

Miguel Alejandro was always known for being very devoted to his studies and sports. At the university, he always stood out for his good conduct and grades; he was also known for being very friendly. Nancy Bustamante, his mother, narrates:

"The last time I saw my son alive was on October 14th, 2002. It was approximately 9:30 in the morning. Miguel was in my bedroom eating some cereal and watching television, before getting ready to study for a midterm exam he had in the coming days. I opened the window of the bedroom in order to let the sunlight in. He smiled. This was the same window through which minutes later entered the stray bullet that would end his life. I went out to run an errand and I left Miguel Alejandro in the apartment with my other son Pablo Andres, who at that moment was sleeping in his bedroom".

Miguel looked out the window for an instant and a bullet from a rifle struck him in the chest. That round had travelled a long distance. According to the District Attorney's CTI, "Crime Scene Investigation Unit", the bullet was at the end of its trajectory because it had lost power and was in a downward spiral due to the force of gravity which was making it fall. It was in that instant when Miguel was at one of the windows of the apartment, in the bullet's trajectory. The wounded young man fell to the ground, from where he started to call out for his brother Pablo to help him.

Pablo Andres, Miguel Alejandro's younger brother narrates:

---

[29] Yarce, Elizabeth. "Streets under fire", In: El Colombiano, Section: Peace and Human Rights, 25th of August, 2002.

"I was sleeping in my bedroom. When suddenly, I heard my brother's screams asking for help. I did not imagine that he had been hit by a bullet, because the shootouts usually took place a long distance away from where we were. For me, it was impossible to think that a bullet could reach my brother from so far away. However, I immediately stood up and left the room to see what was going on. I got to the room where my brother was in a critical condition. I saw him lying on the floor with a lot of blood around him. Desperate, I went outside the apartment screaming and asking for help. I quickly came back to the apartment and tried to lift my brother up, but I was not able to. A few minutes later a neighbor who had heard me screaming for help, came in and helped me take him down from the second floor to the main door of the building, where another neighbor helped us get him in his pickup truck. I sat next to Miguel and we left towards the hospital immediately. My brother, in his death throes, was very nervous and was crying. With a lot of sadness in my heart and tears in my eyes, I told him that he could not leave me, that I loved him a lot. He made a great effort to tell me that he also loved me. I tried to encourage him by telling him that everything was going to be fine and he would recover. A few minutes before reaching the hospital, he stopped responding to what I was saying, but I still hoped that my brother would survive.

At Las Americas Hospital, which is in the Belen neighborhood, he was rushed in right away. After only a few minutes had gone by, the doctor walked towards us and told us that there was nothing more they could do, that he had tried to resuscitate him, but blood had stopped reaching his brain and he was brain dead. I could not stop crying; my older brother, who was my best friend, the person who stood behind me under any circumstance or in any problem I had, had died. It was extremely difficult to have been with him in the last minutes of his life, to watch him die; it was really difficult for us to deal with his death. But it has been much harder to get used to being without him".

His parents' reflection: "Why wait so long to find a solution to a conflict that had been going on for so long? Why not fix it right away and that way save many lives?"

Dealing with the Conflict

One of the youth institutions that served as support for young people who wanted to give peace a chance, so that they would not become victims of the violence, was the YMCA (Young Men's Christian Association.) This organization defines itself as:

A "worldwide movement founded in London in 1844, and that is currently present in more than 120 countries, concentrating its work on education and citizen participation. Its contribution to nonviolent solutions of conflicts has been noted not only in their experience, but also strengthening its capacity and commitment to peace and the involvement of the entire YMCA Worldwide Alliance in support and back-up in areas that are involved in conflict.

In the San Javier headquarters in Comuna 13, the YMCA has worked on building an educational offer focusing on each person´s individual characteristics, promoting their awareness as a legal entity and their participation in social processes to manage local development. There, young people participate in cultural and recreational activities. When the urban conflict flourished in the area, the YMCA served as shelter and a meeting place for many teenagers who on many occasions when leaving school, college or their place of work, could not make it home because of the fighting.

In the middle of the conflict, the YMCA analyzes the facts, expresses its worries and makes its position of nonviolence very clear. It is civil and opposes war, fomenting a yearning for peace, development and the end of armed confrontations.

Nowadays, the YMCA works in five areas: Health promotion, youth organization and participation, education and cohabitation, participative environmental management, and youth entrepreneurship. It also promotes a nonviolent culture. The institution has challenged itself to obtain results with regards to youth in the following areas: self-esteem, adoption of skills and self-care practices, promotion of local development, and non-violent conflict resolution".[30]

Psychologist Manuel Lopez talks about the main problems he perceived in the moments when the conflict in Comuna 13 had worsened, while he worked for the YMCA:

"In Comuna 13, leaders and youth organizations were disintegrating because the conflict disrupted all the groups' dynamics. It was frightening to go outside or to meet and there were orders given by the illegal armed groups, to the effect that no gatherings of people were allowed. There was an attempt to co-opt these youth groups. The rebels used to try to infiltrate these other groups, and invited them to work for the guerilla or to spread their ideas. Most of these youth groups started to split up because of fear.

We had a group of guys at the YMCA who participated in different programs. Our job was to carry out a few projects related to youth organizations, health, and some small financial and educational support work. We used to work hard at finding out what the young people wanted to do by giving them the opportunity to study or to do something productive. The YMCA used to work at that time as an agent of change, as a center where they could go to look for support. At the same

---

[30] Young Men's Christian Association, YMCA, San Javier branch, Medellín, 2004.

time when they showed up, they brought us all the problems that the socio political conflict was causing them, such as the fear, the stigma, the fact that they could not walk freely in their own neighborhoods and many other different issues. Additionally, they brought with them everything related to the place they lived in: poverty, hunger, needs, despair, and a low educational level, amongst many other problems that we had to deal with. We assumed not only the formative educational work that we had been doing with them, but also the emotional work. Many times we had to play the role of listeners, friends, parents, and receive their emotional download, both positive and negative, to calm the rage they felt about the way they had to live. So we contemplated the idea that the site would become a refuge where the guys could go and spend some time. Indeed, our headquarters worked as such during those days; on occasions young people had to stay overnight.

I used to listen to their individual problems and started to discover in these young people something we called post-traumatic stress. Many of them used some psychological skills to free themselves of the pain generated by those types of situations. For example, by turning everything into humor. When there were shootouts in the area, they made jokes and fantasized regarding it. They sarcastically used to say: 'I want to have a gun like that', 'you are from that group', 'I am going to kill you'. But another emotional reaction was denial: 'look, nothing is going on here', 'I have nothing to do with that stuff', 'my life goes on as normal', ' I do not have any problems at all.' The main fear that I used to notice among young people was getting killed by a stray bullet or getting shot because the illegal armed groups mistakenly identified them as being members of the opposing group. Behind all that there was a hidden feeling we called the sense of "no future", an emotion of despair.

I also noticed in young people something we call dysfunctional adaptation to the conflict, according to which the events do not build to any breaking-point in the behavior of the person; instead he or she begins to accept the situation as normal. In general terms, it consists of not reacting to any traumatic situation; for example, not showing indignation when the illegal armed groups killed someone. The only reaction was to curiously take a look. What they would usually say when a person was murdered was; 'He had it coming'. That already shows a certain level of dysfunctional adaptation. Another more extreme way to exhibit this phenomenon consisted of believing that the conflict was valid and that the actions taken by the illegal armed groups were acceptable. So, attacking, mistreating, killing and abusing other people, were ways of adapting, embracing the conflict, assimilating it and making it their own. Not as a victim anymore, but as the victimizer.

Stories of women within the armed conflict

During this conflict, many women were object of multiple aggressions, including rapes and murders. "The dispute between the illegal armed groups (gangs, guerilla and paramilitary) has left them in the middle of the crossfire and it does not matter whether they are fighters or not, they are still persecuted".[31]

Some women who were widows or had been abandoned by their husbands had to make an effort to put food on the table in their households and deal with harassment at the hands of the factions involved in the conflict. The president of a community committee says "it is important to understand the fear that hounds the widows, above all because, after being left to fend for themselves, they are easy prey for violent actors. She notes that many feared being forced to abandon the neighborhood. They are young and they sometimes do not even know if their spouses are group members".[32]

According to a study carried out by the Entre Todos Foundation in 2002, inside the Las Independencias, Nuevos Conquistadores and El Salado neighborhoods, "in 38 of

---

[31] Ospina Zapata, Gustavo. "Young women, confined and without rights", In: El Colombiano, Peace and Human Rights Section, Medellín, May 18th, 2002.

[32] Ospina Zapata, Gustavo. "Widows and orphans live with the consequences of the urban conflict", In: El Colombiano, Peace and Human Rights Section, Medellín, May 3rd, 2002.

every 100 families, the head of the household is a woman, which shows that they are the ones who have to work and carry the responsibility of survival on their shoulders".[33]

Many women from the area avoided getting involved with members of the illegal armed groups as much as they could. Others had to give in to the demands of such people in order to avoid becoming victims of their aggressions. But others got involved with some of the members simply because they felt attracted or protected by them.

Women Members of Illegal Armed Groups

Some women were members of the illegal groups involved in the conflict. They took part in armed confrontations and occasionally in criminal activities: "they are no longer only mothers, girlfriends, or sisters of the members of a gang or armed group, but now they are taking part in the war".[34]

Karen[*] is a young lady who lived in the Las Independencias neighborhood and was a member of the CAP and ELN guerillas for a period of two years:

"I used to like to party, but every time I wanted to go out I had problems with my parents, because they did not like me going out. In those days, the dominant group in the neighborhood used to be the Carlos Alirio Buitrago group of the ELN, but they called themselves Los Regionales or The Regionals in English. My sister became the girlfriend of one of them and all three

---

[33] Ospina Zapata, Gustavo. "Comuna 13: death and oblivion", In: El Colombiano, Peace and Human Rights Section, Medellín, October 10th, 2002.

[34] Perez Gonzales, Paula. "Women victims of the conflict and crime". In: El Colombiano, October 16th, 2003, p. 11A

[*] Name changed to protect her identity.

of us started going out together. Since my mother was quite scared of them, she did not prohibit me. In one of those outings, I met one of the bosses of the CAP and started dating him. He convinced me to join their organization. I was 17 years old, and there I felt protected and respected. In my house no one would say anything to me anymore. I used to go once or twice a week to get clothes and then return to sector 3 in the La Independencia neighborhood. The girls used to respect and fear me.

I started out as an informer. I used to inform them who was stealing or talking bad about them. To tell the truth, in those days I enjoyed what I was doing. Once an ELN commander arrived from the rural area of the municipality of Campamento and told my boyfriend that I had to show my courage and needed to go to the jungle. So I went with the plan of staying for a year but three months later I came back because I could not handle it there. It turns out that what the commander wanted was to sleep with me. Other women within the organization told me that if I accepted him, I would be able to do whatever I wanted, and that is why I consented. But that was not the case: I still had to pull guard anyway. On the contrary, it was worse, because that guy used to arrive there early in the morning and would send someone to relieve me, but only so I could have sex with him. After that I could not sleep because we had to get up at four in the morning to study politics, practice shooting at targets and carry firewood, among other obligations. I suffered a lot, because in the jungle I used to work day and night. When we came back to town I had the opportunity to speak with my mother and told her to talk to my boyfriend so he could ask to have me back again, that I could show my bravery in the city. I did not have any problems, since the commander had already gotten what he wanted, so he sent me back to Medellín. When I came back to the city on February 2001, `the clean-ups` which were indiscriminate murders against the homeless, drug addicts and thieves, intensified in Comuna 13. I unfortunately witnessed the murder of friends who I grew up with. They always went with some women to stash their weapons when they were going down to Veinte de Julio neighborhood or the cemetery.

In my neighborhood, I earned the hatred of my friends and neighbors, there was a time when no one would speak to me; if they did, it was out of fear of me taking some form of retaliation against them. My fears were that the paramilitary group would take over the neighborhood, getting killed or ending up in jail.

I retired from the ELN in November 2001, when they killed a commander who used to help us a lot. I did not have anywhere to go, so I had to stay at my parents' house, facing the consequences of my actions. In fact, I was locked up in the El Buen Pastor Jail for six months. After the military operation Orion, I used to live in horrible fear, because even though it had been more than a year since I had retired from the ELN, I still had death threats against me. On one occasion I had to stay away from my house for eight days, and other times I had to hide in the dirty clothes hamper. I lived like that until John Chiqui got killed, a paramilitary member who had been in the guerillas and who was the one looking for me to murder me.

To the young people who are living through a similar situation to the one I experienced, I would ask them to reconsider and abandon it, not to waste the opportunity to live again, to make up with society and their families, because family is the only thing that will be behind them through all good and bad situations. I joined the illegal armed groups in part because in my house I used to get told what to do and also told off. I hope that young people can realize that in the guerillas you do not only get told off, but also hit and even killed or executed if you do not obey an order.

To the ones who are thinking about joining an illegal armed group, I tell them not to let themselves be fooled, because everything they say is a lie. There, you are worse off than in jail. You never do what you want; only what they tell you to do. You never get any financial incentives to help your family, because everything is kept by the commanders. If you are a woman, you get a little bit luckier, but only if the commanders like you, because with women the popular saying applies "for one and for all"; you must go to bed with first one commander and then another. Later on, you are the same as everyone, or maybe worse, pulling shifts: you go hungry because you do not always have something to eat, especially if the Army is in the area.

As a combatant, you risk your life for the commanders at every moment; and what do they do? They leave. In a risky situation, they are the ones taken out of the area first, and they let the dummies die. If you are over there and your family interferes too much, you have to turn them in so they can be killed, just for telling you to wish to be out, because that is their law. Whoever screws up, pays for it.

If you end up in jail, sometimes they do not even contribute enough money to pay for a lawyer. And if you are lucky, they send you 60.000 pesos [Equivalent to approximately $24 USD at the time] every month for personal items. But the 'dons' (commanders), if you visit one of them in jail, you will find they have all the amenities. As a matter of fact, they are not even housed in the so called political prisoners block.

While I was in the guerilla, many young people joined to feel protected by a gun, not because of an ideology or money, because it does not exist there. Whoever is the leader is the one who takes all. The rest of the people just do the dirty work, get enemies, and lose their families, friends and even their lives".

After getting out of jail, Karen went back to the Las Independencias neighborhood. Sometime later, an illegal armed group tried to kill her. Since they didn't accomplish their objective, they murdered her father and afterwards her husband. That is why she abandoned the area with her son.

Many women served as part of the illegal armed factions carrying out intelligence and surveillance work or moving firearms from or to Comuna 13 because as women they were less likely to be seen as suspects. Alejandra*, a young woman who lived in the Veinte de Julio neighborhood and who was a member of the CAP urban guerilla, narrates:

"Before joining the group, I had a boyfriend who was in the organization. He did not tell me to join because he was a very prudent fellow. He was one of the top guys in the group and directed operations in part of the El Salado neighborhood.

I started hanging out with more of the young people in the CAP and I became friends with a girl. I used to hang out with them all the time, some of them used to tell me that it was really good. Others used to tell me that this life style was good for nothing, because of the long nights and that it was very dangerous.

Out of curiosity and keeping true to that popular adage ‛in life you must try a bit of everything`, I started receiving political training from them, without my boyfriend knowing. When he found out, he asked me why I was there, and told me that I should not do it because I had two kids. However, I did not listen, because I felt protected, as the brother of a lady who lived in the same place as me tried to take advantage of me sexually. He did not do it because I threatened to report him to the guerillas. Also, I wanted respect, because many women in the neighborhood did not like me. I thought that by being in the guerillas those girls would not mess with me. I did not take the consequences which it could bring me into account. I thought that the guerilla was never going to be forced out of the neighborhood, that just could not happen.

---

* Name changed to protect her identity.

With respect to the weapons, I used to keep them, but I did not use to permanently carry one or ever use them against anyone. Mostly I was used for taking stuff such as medicine to them and also for taking care of the sick members of the organization.

Once, I went with my boyfriend to a wooden shack. At that time the Army and District Attorney's unit were on the outskirts and a terrible shootout could be heard. There was no way out anywhere. I was shaking with fear. I was not thinking that I would end up in jail; I thought I was going to die. `Today is the day`, I was thinking and crying; my boyfriend kept telling me: `relax, calm down; they are not going to catch us`. I responded: `Look at the house full of weapons, there is no way out. Nobody can get away from here`. However, they were not able to get into that house even though they passed near it, and the next day everything had become calm again.

The most difficult thing about being in the organization was that I could not spend much time with my children anymore. Neither see them every day nor stay in one house too long.

During the military operation Orion, I used to think since I had not done anyone any harm, I did not have any reason to flee. I did not try to leave the neighborhood, even though many of the guerilla members had already left. In those days I went to work at the Antonio Nariño neighborhood. While I was there, someone knocked on the door; when I opened, there were several police officers outside, but I did not think they were there for me. `How can I help you? `, I asked them. They told me to go with them, `Where? ` I asked in fear while laughing. My boss came out and asked them what was going on. The police officers told him that I had to go with them, that I was not a criminal, but that I knew many things which could help them. I told the officers to wait so I could get ready. I went inside and I organized myself and left my number with a woman. I told her to call my children's grandmother, and to let my roommate know what was going on; when I got to the Sijin (Judicial Police), my friend whom I lived with, was already there: they had taken her in first.

My family paid a lawyer for me. After eight days in a cell at the police station, they transferred me to the women's jail, indicted for rebellion, and seven months later I was released. Afterwards, I moved away from Comuna 13 and my friends".

Community Leaders

Even in the face of all the adversities, "women have demonstrated an invaluable ability of leadership and appropriation, and have made all their common knowledge available in the service of their communities, a legacy which still remains even though they have become victims of the conflict, widows, mothers who cry over their children's graves, etc".[35]

During the conflict, women played a vital socioeconomic role in this comuna. One example that stands out is AMI the Las Independencias Women's Association, an organization that was born in 1996 and became a reality in the AMIGA (Girlfriend) house, a place set up and owned by the association thanks to the efforts of its members who through diverse projects have contributed to generating a place of learning, development and meeting for the women from Veinte de Julio, Las Independencias, El Salado and Nuevos Conquistadores neighborhoods.

During the confrontation, many of the association's women were directly affected by the actions of the armed groups involved in the conflict. Nowadays, lots of them give thanks to a woman who through a hard and painstaking struggle on top of behind the scenes labor –for that not less

---

[35] Diagnostic Report on the Socioeconomic and Conflict situation in Comuna 13. Government of Medellín, October 2002, p. 14.

Photograph: Fredy Amariles, El Mundo Newspaper.

meritorious- prevented something many saw as imminent: the disappearance of AMI. This woman, one of the founding members of this NGO was Inés Jiménez; she has lived in Veinte de Julio neighborhood since 1983. She states: "Despite all the sweat, the pain and the blood, we had to fight not to die trying and in the end we were able to achieve it".

Some other women stood out during the conflict for their work in the search for improvement of the quality of life of the people who had settled in the area. Others stood out for risking their lives, intervening on behalf of people who had been sentenced to death by the illegal armed groups, in order to get them to pardon their lives.

One of these women was Carla*, a Las Independencias neighborhood resident, who contributed to saving lives in the area. Occasionally, when the illegal armed groups came down with people they were going to kill, she interceded on their behalf so that they would not harm them, sometimes being successful in her pretensions and thus saving their lives. In some cases, despite her pleas, the illegal armed group members went ahead and murdered their victims. Frequently, members of the illegal armed groups would accuse her of getting involved in matters that were none of her business, according to them, and although her life at times could have been in danger, that was not a good enough reason for her to become scared or quit helping save lives:

"One time, while sleeping at home, I woke up. It was three in the morning and I heard someone arguing. I stood up and stepped out on the balcony. I saw four men who had a boy next to the door of my house and he was insulting them a lot.

I had never seen anyone stand up to them like that; he did not stop insulting and threatening them. They were angry from

---

* Name changed to protect her identity.

seeing that kid who was saying such things to them and who did not show any fear. They were pushing him and saying: 'shut up you piece of shit, shut up or we are going to kill you, you do not know who you are talking to'. The boy told them: 'Yes, I know who I am talking to: you are the guerilla, and I am a *paraco'**. He did not seem scared at that moment, but he was really angry. He did not once beg them not to hurt him, instead every time they told him that they were going to kill him, he became rowdier and insulted them.

I ran downstairs between the men and I asked them not to hurt him; then I asked one of the men: 'Hey dude, what›s going on? Why is that boy saying that to you? ' He told me: 'Ah! This son of a bitch is challenging us; he is high, out of his mind, and he knows he can`t be using drugs over here, or be in the streets, and besides that, we are telling him off and he keeps insulting us'.

So I said to them: 'Take it easy, can`t you see he is just a kid? He is stoned right now and does not know what he is saying'. One of them responded: 'That motherfucker does know what he is saying to us, because if he is treating us that way, it is because he knows'.

I told the man to let me speak to the boy, and he responded: 'Ah! Ok, take care of him, but that son of a bitch can`t stay here; tomorrow we have to know where he is from'.

I took the boy inside the house and we stayed there until 06:00 in the morning, because I was worried that he might go after them. I told him to calm down, and asked him why he said such things. He told me that they had killed his father two years ago and he was never going to forgive them for that. They had also taken his family's house and made them leave the neighborhood.

** Popular name given to members of the paramilitary groups.

I asked him his age and he told me he was thirteen. He told me that, one day when the whole family was at home in the La Independencia neighborhood, those men came in, took the family outside and killed his father in front of everyone, supposedly because he was a drug addict. He said that, even though his father was addicted, it was not right for them to have murdered him because he worked and did not steal from anyone, so there was no reason for them to have killed him for that motive. So he thought that it could have been because they had a grudge against their family.

He told me that they had moved to the El Bosque neighborhood; once there, he had run into problems with some hoodlums. So his mother had sent him back to live with his aunt in the La Independencia neighborhood.

At six o'clock that morning, I left my house and headed to his family's home. I spoke to his aunt and she told me that ever since his father's death, the boy had started to use drugs and hang out on the streets. She also told me that he was now responsible for providing for his mother and brother, and in order to do so, he sold candies on buses.

Later in the afternoon, the guerilla members came back and I told them: 'You have to understand that you have killed people, and that is why there are people in the area who hold grudges against you.'

They got in contact with the boy's aunt and told her that it would be better if she took him out of the neighborhood to avoid getting himself killed because, according to them, even though he was only a boy, because of his way of thinking, he posed a threat and, therefore, was considered an enemy".

Medical and Aid Groups

The medical mission was quite affected by the armed conflict in Comuna 13. Healthcare workers were often the victims of kidnappings and intimidations. Moreover, some of their premises and vehicles were hit by bullets. Such was the case with the San Javier Medical Center building and an ambulance belonging to Metrosalud in the Veinte de Julio neighborhood. Luckily, no one was hurt in these incidents.

There were times when the employees were trapped inside the aid centers because of the constant confrontations which took place among the different armed factions and many times they had to lie down on the floor for hours in order to avoid getting struck by bullets.

Sometimes, healthcare workers had to go to work at the health centers in the middle of the shootouts, risking their own lives in order to save others. Since there were constant emergencies, no healthcare worker could miss even one day of work. As a matter of fact, on several occasions, they had to work overtime or, after a long shift, had to stay overnight in the health center because there was still shooting going on in the area and it was too risky to leave. Additionally, there were instances when because of the worsening of confrontations, healthcare workers had to be transported to work in Police or Army armored troop carrying vehicles, to avoid being wounded.

Though healthcare workers used to make an initial evaluation of patients in order to figure out who needed faster care according to the gravity of their wounds, there were moments when they were intimidated by members of the armed groups, so their comrades would be taken care of first, even if there were other civilian patients with more severe wounds who required urgent care "Something like that happened to a doctor who worked at the health center in the La Quiebra neighborhood, one night when he had to take care of a guerilla member with a bullet wound. `You either save him or you die´, was the ultimatum that one of the wounded man's comrades gave him, while pointing a gun at his face".[36]

Jaime[*] is a doctor, who, after working in different health centers of the northeast region of the city, was transferred to the La Loma medical center on June 22nd, 2000. While working there he experienced several difficult situations:

"Starting in the year 2000, we began to be directly affected by the armed conflict. One day we were detained for an hour and a half by an armed group inside the health center. During that time, one of the employees went to answer the phone, and one of the gunmen pointed a gun at her head and made her hang up. She was terrified and started crying. That same day, they shot from inside the aid center at another armed group that was on the outside near the La Loma church, with us trapped inside the aid center in the crossfire. Luckily we were not hurt.

On some occasions, we were overwhelmed by the presence of gunmen who brought their wounded or sick to the aid center. Once inside, they intimidated us and made the healthcare personnel take care of their people immediately; there was a lot of fear because no one knew who they were or what they were there for. For us as healthcare workers, we must not

---

[36] Aricapa, Ricardo. Comuna 13: Chronicles of an urban war. Second Edition, p.187, Universidad de Antioquia, Editorial, Medellín, 2005.

[*] Name changed to protect his identity.

consider a person's beliefs, political allegiance, color, religion, or anything else when it comes to doing our job; every person that shows up must be taken care of.

One day, on my way to work at about six in the morning, I saw a lot of people wearing ski masks and carrying long range weapons near the medical center as I arrived on the bus. I kept walking but fearing that I would be shot in the back. A few moments after entering the center, a big gunfight broke out in the area and I had to stay inside for about five hours, lying on the floor the whole time. From management in the town hall, Metrosalud sent someone in a vehicle to take me out of the area. He arrived at about eleven in the morning; in order to get there, he had to go through the San Cristobal sector because it was impossible to cross San Javier.

At home, I used to tell my family that I was going to work but I was not sure if I would make it back, because there was always the risk that I could be killed. We did not have anything to do with the conflict; we were simply healthcare workers who had turn up for our job in the area.

On September 17th, 2002, the dentist and a dental assistant were detained when they were passing by the San Javier Medical Center. Following this incident, on October 3rd, four other Metrosalud employees and I were kidnapped by an illegal armed group who demanded two million pesos from us, [Equivalent to approximately $798 USD at the time] in exchange for our freedom. They let us go after detaining us for four hours, but only after we paid the amount of money they demanded.

On the other hand, among the residents of the area that we took care of at the La Loma health center on a daily basis, we noticed many people with anxiety, insomnia, gastric ulcers, chronic tension and all types of headaches, because the daily dose of violence affected them a lot. Women had more rooted symptoms and showed more nervousness. We perceived that all these physical and psychological symptoms were more frequently evident in residents during the time of the armed conflict in the area".

At the medical center in San Javier, healthcare workers laid face down on the ground as soon as they heard shooting nearby. They carried communication radios, and also kept mats, blankets and something to eat in case they had to spend the night at the center. Furthermore, they had a back door built so they could evacuate rapidly if they had to. Ana*, a nurse at the medical center in San Javier neighborhood, says:

"About the sector, I can say that it was a community with huge social problems and many needs. Back in 2002, the law

and order situation in the area was quite critical for us the healthcare workers in San Javier; we started to be directly affected on May 21st. That day, while I was on the bus on my way to start my shift at seven in the morning, I saw groups of Police and Army troops moving in the area, and shooting was also heard. The bus did not pass in front of the aid center as usual, instead dropping us off in front of the Metro station. I felt anguish and fear from not knowing what was going on. However, I walked towards the aid center in order to start working and assisting my colleagues. I imagined that there had been showdowns between the illegal armed groups and government forces since the early hours of the morning.

When I got to the unit, I found my colleagues who had worked the nightshift completely drained. They told me that the confrontations had started in the area at one in the morning. They were supposed to finish their shift at seven in the morning that day, but stayed a few more hours to help us.

That whole day was a nightmare for us. I counted thirty-five people wounded and nine deaths on my shift; among the dead there were four children. I remember that the stretcher bearer came in with a young girl who had gotten hit in the

---

* Name changed to protect her identity.

head by a bullet shot from a rifle; the bullet had completely destroyed her head. The guy was pulling his own hair, crying and screaming desperately when he came in with her. I told him to cover her body with a sheet. I had never seen a wound produced by a rifle round. It was terrifying to see what it had done to that girl. We were not able to do anything to save her life. I had never cried so much as I did that day. The situation was too critical, and I was not able to cope with such dramatic conditions. In those moments of anguish, we hugged each other and cried even in front of the patients. We used to console each other, because even though we were competent at our work, we were full of fear and sadness. Besides the patients wounded by gunfire, we also treated other patients who required general medical attention. So, when a poor old lady came in with cardiorespiratory arrest, and several people with bullet wounds, some of them in really bad shape, we had to quickly analyze which patient deserved priority.

There were officials from the District Attorney's Office, Police, Army, and other government agencies, as well as family members of the wounded. I was one of the people who made everyone respect the neutrality of the hospital. When someone would park a Police or Army vehicle in front of the medical center, I immediately asked them to move it away from there. I used to do it for our own safety, so as not to give the illegal armed groups a reason to attack us. A doctor from the Fourth Army Brigade offered to help us take care of patients, but I refused her assistance. I told her that I did not have anything against the Army, but we wanted to remain neutral in the conflict. However, that objective was not enough because in the afternoon, when the shootings had ceased and the members of the government forces had left the area, some armed teenagers came into the aid center, they looked to be about fourteen and fifteen years old on average. One of them threatened us by saying that if they found even one police officer inside, they would kill us. At that time, I was so overwhelmed and tired because of the tragic situation we had experienced that day that I did not control my words and told him: 'Show some respect, do not be so defiant and rude. Get out of here'. Even though the guy had a weapon, I did not feel fear. What I felt was anger, because I did not want any more aggression, deaths, and I did not want to be confronted. After searching the entire health center and not finding what they were looking for, they departed.

We continued to hear the shooting in the area during the following days. Many times, when there were confrontations in the area, we had to call the homes of the workers from the aid centers to tell them who had to work the night shift; they had to start their shifts later that night. Those who had worked all day had to wait until they got to work before we could leave.

Conditions carried on being very dramatic. We began to receive threats against us. There was a rumor going round that they were going to use an explosive device to blow up the aid center, because we were a government institution. According to them, we were supporting the Government Forces. On one occasion, they shot at the aid center and we all got really scared. We called management to inform about what was going on and they told us that we could not abandon our place of work. I was really frightened and called my sister to tell her that they were going to kill us in the health center. The next day, we called the media to denounce the fact that all of us healthcare workers were working at the aid center without any security measures in the place. We demanded respect towards the medical mission from the armed groups because we were impartial in the conflict. I also told the aid center's director to please order an alternative exit to be built in the back of the building, so we eventually would be able to use it, when the shootouts were taking place.

Since there were already threats, every time we heard shooting we used to think they were going to come into the aid center to take us. There was a lot of panic, so much so, that the social worker could not take it anymore and requested to be transferred.

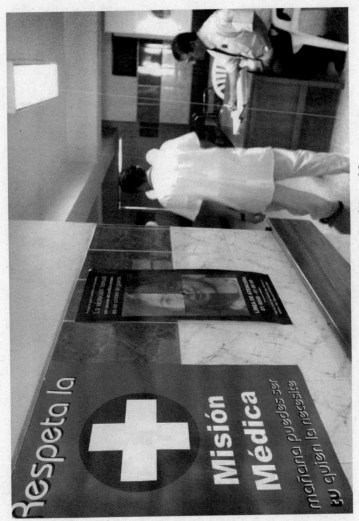

Photograph: Jaime Pérez, El Colombiano Newspaper.

Apart from all that, I was really struck by seeing on some occasions corpses lying on the ground outside in plain sight and that continued for a long time because the authorities could not come into the area to process the scenes. This was due to the fact that every time the coroner's office officials would show up to process a crime scene as such, they would always be shot at. Usually, it was the Police who would end up having to process the crime scenes that involved dead bodies.

One of the most horrifying things was that sometimes we had to stack up to four or five corpses in a bathroom we had reserved for intoxicated people. Generally, there were bodies left there by taxi drivers who were forced by the illegal armed groups to take away the corpses inside their trunks. We used to tell the taxi drivers to take them directly to the morgue, but they would not dare go through the city with a dead body inside their cars, especially because they could be accused of the crime themselves. So we had to take them and stack them up in that room, until the police arrived to pick them up. This was a health problem for us.

During that year, we suffered from an increase in back pain, headaches, anxiety and depression. Constantly, we listened the stories of residents of the area who came for regular medical visits; these stories made us more fearful and nervous. They would tell us about all types of problems they were having in the area where they lived, such as the death of a family member, friend, or someone they knew, or the forced displacement of one of the families in the neighborhood by the illegal armed groups.

Residents of the area were fed up with the conflict. You could see people walking on the street in front of the aid center, right in the middle of the shootings, as if their lives were not at risk at that moment. I remember a man who had left his job and was on his way home at the same time that there was a battle taking place. When he passed by I said to him: 'Sir, can't you see that they are shooting? Do not keep going! That person responded: 'I am really hungry, and I am going home' I told him: 'Look, you can be wounded if you go that way' and he said: 'It does not matter, I cannot take this, every day, anymore', and continued on towards his house".

***

It is well known that "[...] the role that, for example, the Fire Department, the Civil Defense, the Simpad, first aid and rescue organizations, as well as Empresas Publicas and Empresas Varias by extension, play in El Valle del Aburrá, is protected under International Human Rights".[37] However, members of the illegal armed groups assaulted members of aid organizations and forbid them from entering some areas of Comuna 13, threatening to kill them if they went inside those areas to help.

Juan Hurtado, who works for the Fire Department of Medellín, narrates what he and three other colleagues experienced while they were putting out a forest fire:

"At about two in the afternoon on March 4th, 2002, we were dispatched to Comuna 13 in order to put out a forest fire. After working to extinguish the fire for about forty minutes, a group of approximately forty gunmen showed up on the scene. They insulted us, threw us on the floor and detained us. They terrorized the firetruck driver by making him open his mouth and placing a weapon inside it, but they did not hurt him. On several occasions they insinuated that they were going to kill us. One of my colleagues tried to flee, but he was caught and beaten. Those people stripped us of our working tools and had us detained for approximately twenty-five minutes. When they let us go, they warned us not to come back to that place".

---

[37] Arboleda García, Javier. "Harakiri in the urban conflict", In: El Colombiano Newspaper, Medellín, October 13th, 2002.

Voices of Hope

In the face of so much injustice and suffering, religious leaders offered a voice of hope. In an area where there were many people longing for timely peace, but at the same time, people who imposed their way by using terror and overwhelming firepower, priests and preachers urged the population to face every difficult situation with courage through prayer.

Some religious leaders had to devise ways to hold worship services in each sector, because people were not allowed to freely cross over from one place to another: illegal armed groups applied certain restrictions to people's freedom of movement in many of the neighborhoods of Comuna 13. Residents of the areas where the guerillas had presence were not supposed to walk around in areas controlled by paramilitary groups or vice versa; if they did, they would be at risk of being murdered. That is why some religious leaders, like priest Roberto Seguín from Blanquizal neighborhood church scheduled mass in different sectors so the residents of each area would not have to risk their lives going to church.

Priest Roberto Seguin was born on April 2nd, 1940 in Detroit USA, where he also grew up and went to school. He studied theology in Toronto and served as chaplain at the University of Windsor in Canada. After that, he worked in Indiana and was ordained in 1969. For a while he taught religion in New York. He also studied biochemistry for five years in Windsor, Canada, where he had the opportunity to teach chemistry and biology for some time as well as in Detroit, USA. After that, he was the priest at a church in Houston, Texas. He belongs to the Basilian Priests Congregation of San Basilio, a community founded in France during the French Revolution by a group of diocesan priests, and whose purpose is to educate and evangelize. He relates his experience in Comuna 13, during some of the most critical moments:

"A group of the Basilian Priests Congregation was looking for someone who would want to come to Colombia with the objective of having a presence in the area, especially in the areas which have suffered the most from violence and poverty. I did not speak Spanish, so at that moment it never crossed my mind that this would be part of my story. However, I got to Colombia in 1986, precisely to learn Spanish and analyze if it would be possible for me to stay. I studied in Bogota for three months; after that I went back to the United States and continued working at the church. The next year, I came back to Colombia. I spoke very little Spanish and I did not know much about the conflict inside the country. The change was very difficult for me but, despite everything, I think it was what God wanted for me.

I lived in Cali city for eight years, precisely in the Agua Blanca District, where many people spoke to me about family members who had died because of the violence. I learned many things during that time. Above all, I learned to value the Colombian people, who with so much courage and faith have forgiven and decided not to take revenge. The conflict would be worse if these people decided to retaliate. Meeting people who had really decided not to seek revenge impressed me a lot.

I arrived at Medellín City in 1996. I was in the Prado Centro neighborhood for a year, and the next year the Archbishop of Medellín showed me several sectors to work in. I chose to work with Priest Pedro Miguel Mora at a small church called Ecce Homo, in Blanquizal neighborhood of Comuna 13.

It was very quiet the first year, but the problems began the following one: conflicts between illegal armed groups from two different neighborhoods. In order to decrease tensions, we used to try to mediate between the two sides.

With support from the Social Pastoral of the Archdiocese of Medellín, we began working with youth, by starting a workshop called "San Basilio, youth art". The idea was to offer these people an alternative to violence and conflict. We had 30 teenagers involved in the project at that time. They used to make handicrafts and then would go out to sell them at different churches. We emphasized to them the importance of education and getting ahead.

As time went by, in the years 2001 and 2002, the conflict got worse and dozens of people were murdered in the Blanquizal and Olaya Herrera neighborhoods. As a consequence, many kids were turned into orphans and numerous women into widows. It was very sad to have to perform so many funeral rites. I shared in the sadness and pain of many families that had lost loved ones, and we were forced to initiate social and spiritual guidance work with many of these victims of the violence. We also continued trying to mediate between the different armed groups in the area with the purpose of decreasing the tension as much as possible.

On many occasions, as I was coming into the neighborhood, I got trapped in the crossfire while the different armed groups were shooting at each other. I remember one time as I was entering the Blanquizal neighborhood in the church's vehicle, the streets were deserted. Subsequently, I heard the blast of an explosive artifact not too far from where I was, and then the shooting started. I sped up the vehicle until I got to the church amidst all the crossfire.

Another day, I was with some children in front of the church, when suddenly we felt the buzzing sound of a bullet which passed above us, very close, and impacted the church's wall.

147

I used to celebrate mass many times in the street but because of the conflict, there were occasions when we would find ourselves trapped amidst the bullets. We also saw people with guns walking among the attendees, which used to generate fear and tension for us and the people who attended mass.

During the armed conflict, with the help of some churchgoers, we had to pick up thirteen corpses of people who had been murdered and I took them from the streets to the municipal morgue in the church's vehicle. I also took many people who had been wounded in the neighborhood to the aid centers. I used to do this because no one else dared to pick up the corpses or the wounded, out of fear of becoming the target of attacks by the armed groups. Sometimes, while doing this, we risked our lives by exposing ourselves in the middle of the shootouts.

I thought the conflict was absurd and senseless, and even though we were threatened once, I never tried to leave the country. I found courage in each difficult situation, and that's how I have continued to preach about Jesus. I speak about his forgiveness from the cross, and I ask people to continue on the path of forgiveness instead of taking revenge, as part of their personal liberation. I always preach faith and Christ's forgiveness, teaching about how he, through his mercy, forgave our sins. I ask every person not to opt for the path of revenge because this path only generates more violence and suffering. I know it is very hard but only by forgiving is the spirit of vengeance expelled".

Rafael Orlando Jaramillo, a priest who has worked in the Nazareth Church of the El Corazon neighborhood since December 3rd, 2001, talks about his experiences in the middle of the conflict:

"I have always worked in places that require a lot of spiritual help and accompaniment. With regards to the situation experienced at the church, well I arrived there when there were many difficulties.

At first, I felt powerless in relation to the conflict. I did not know which way to go, but through prayer, and thanks to God, I was able to persevere and move ahead, certainly through the gospel, which is the teaching par excellence that shows that Jesus makes himself real and more alive; that gospel, which, in each critical and painful moment that we go through, live and feel is always that open letter to love, and to teach the population that they have to live in peace here, to be bearers of peace; and that when faced with the reality of death, this could not be repaid with more death, or responded to with the same harm.

Several people who had lost loved ones in the conflict used to tell me that they were not able to suppress their feelings of vengeance, so I addressed them through my sermons and talked directly with them through confession. After so many words and consolation, many people began to reconsider their ways and ended up understanding that things could not continue down the same path.

Something that affected me a lot was, when one day before starting mass, some people came to me and told me that many aspects of the sermon had to be changed, because I spoke too openly. So I felt scared, but 'I put myself in the hands of the Lord', went up to the pulpit and celebrated mass. It seems that these people wanted to control the work that was being done a bit, the fact that I was speaking openly to people and questioning the position churchgoers should take in regards to the violence.

Another day, some people got inside the church because they were looking for someone specific; it seemed with the intention of killing that person, and they thought that is where that person was at the time. We did not know what to do, we just hid until it was all over. When we went to the church, there was no one there but they had damaged the sacristy door. My God! Can you imagine how it was when they went to someone's house to kill a person? They would probably kill the person right in front of their family. It is painful and tragic; my opinion is that only through that voice of consolation and hope can people get ahead, despite all the critical situations.

Now, when I look back and see the faces in pain, families destroyed, and the community marginalized because of so many things that happened, all I can say is: how were we able to get through that? We were only able to get through it by the power of God".

Mario Castrillon Restrepo, the parish priest at the Veinte de Julio neighborhood church, relates his experience amidst the conflict:

"I arrived at the Veinte de Julio neighborhood on January 30th, 2001, right in the middle of a shootout, to perform the funeral rites for a person who had been murdered. I abstained from making a pastoral plan in many sectors because of the constant shootouts that took place in those areas. The illegal armed groups only allowed us to perform mass, which was really helpful and provided much needed support for the community.

In prayer, we used to ask for God's intervention so that men would change their violent mentality and stop their criminal behavior. I used to provide a word of encouragement to churchgoers so they would go on without losing faith and they would feel that they were not alone, that God himself was a victim of the conflict, and that by uniting ourselves to his suffering on the cross, we could handle the difficulties with faith. The illegal armed groups never agreed with the sermons because they felt it touched on their bad actions. My greatest fears were:

- Express kidnappings: kidnapped victims' family members asked for my help, and I could not do anything about it.

- Seeing defenseless people being brought down from the higher sector of the neighborhood, with their hands tied, looking like lambs being taken to the slaughter house, and killed in the presence of the population.

- The conflict became part of the folklore. Many people became desensitized to others suffering. Someone getting killed had become common.

- Accompanying so many funerals of children and teenagers, murdered frequently, used to hurt me a lot.

- I thought it was quite sad to see so many minors as members of the illegal armed groups. In some cases, their weapons were bigger than they were".

The testimonies of these priests coincide with a chronicle in the De la Urbe newspaper:

"A scream interrupted the service at the La Divina Pastora temple in the El Salado neighborhood. The priest was trying to keep everyone calm while a masked gunman pointed a firearm at his head. It was a little after seven in the evening on a Sunday in February 2002, and the people who had gathered to take part in the most important religious moment of the week were stunned at seeing their priest being subdued by this man.

Although there were no deaths or shots fired in El Salado that night, a poor neighborhood up in the hills that surround Medellín on its west side, the fact that the war between the guerilla and paramilitary groups would be to the death was made public by this action. The masked gunman announced there with very strong words that his group was prepared to fight without stopping and that everyone there was part of the war".[38]

Due to the mission of the Roman Catholic Church in making a contribution to peace in the area, the priests became targets of

---

[38] De la Urbe Newspaper No. 15, "Overwhelmed by war". Communications Faculty Universidad de Antioquia, August, 2002, p. 9.

attacks by the illegal armed groups on several occasions. They were threatened and even killed.

This was the case of 48-year-old Father Jose Luis Arroyave Restrepo who, amid the furor of the conflict, used to mediate between the different illegal armed groups, taking his message of peace and hope to them in order to avoid so much bloodshed in the area; and who also used to dedicate much of his time and effort to the less fortunate among the people. He was one of the organizers of the march for life and non-violence, which took place on June 9th, 2002 in Comuna 13, and was able to gather more than 4,000 people. According to a forum directed by the El Colombiano newspaper, "Priest Jose Luis Arroyave, the charismatic community leader, well known and loved in Comuna 13, denounces the hunger that exists in the area. But not only hunger for food, also for knowledge and a will to live, which is the hunger that people desperately have. He points out that the comuna needs a large investment in equity and social justice and that instead of militarizing the area it must be humanized".[39]

On the other hand, in a newspaper article, some of his last statements are remembered: "Jose Luis Arroyave was referred to as an Apostle of the poor. During a forum on urban conflict which was organized by El Colombiano newspaper a few days before his death, he stated: 'Dead or alive, I give my life for Comuna 13' ".[40]

As if these words were a premonition: on September 20th, 2002, in the Juan XXIII neighborhood, members of an illegal armed group shot him several times, causing his death. This is how priest Arroyave's life came to an end. He is also remembered in the city as the Apostle of Peace or a martyr of Comuna 13.

---

[39] Aricapa, Ricardo. Comuna 13: Chronicles of an urban war. Second Edition, p. 194. Universidad de Antioquia, Editorial, Medellín, 2005.

[40] Yarce, Elizabeth. "Father Arroyave's work recognized in Holland". In: El Colombiano, Section: Peace and Human Rights. Medellín, November 22nd, 2002.

"Causes" of the conflict according to the combatants

Knowing what motivated some people to take up arms and directly participate in the conflict could help us understand why the armed conflict in Comuna 13 had such significance. However, this is difficult to establish because each member of the illegal armed groups used different reasoning to justify all the atrocities they committed against the civilian population and members of enemy groups; and their actions that were usually violations of human rights and International Humanitarian Rights law.

Alias Corolo*, who was a member of the ELN's urban unit in Comuna 13, and who was incarcerated at the maximum security unit of Itagüí's jail, talks about some of the motives that made him join that organization.

"Since it was impossible for one to walk from block to block because you would get attacked, the Villa Laura neighborhood where I lived was not safe at all. John Chiqui, a man I knew, who had been a member of the ELN in the past, got several young guys together, including me, and started a group called FRAP Antiparamilitary Revolutionary Group.

We started by learning about Marxist-Leninist political theories and taking care of the neighborhood. In December 1998, members of the ELN's Luis Fernando Giraldo Builes urban front sent a message to us, saying that we had to join their organization or they would kill us. None of us opted to

---

* Name changed to protect his identity.

join them, so we started a war with them and they killed a guy nicknamed The Indian and wounded other members of the FRAP.

The ELN took over the neighborhood and our group was finished. A few days later they called me; I showed up and they told me to work with them or to leave the neighborhood. My answer was that I did not work for anybody, so a couple of days later I decided to join the Army, and was there until December 2000. When I got back, the neighborhood was organized differently. There was a lot of guerilla, and since I did not have a job, I was in a difficult financial situation, dealing with the fact that my wife was about to give birth in a few weeks. Therefore, I accepted the help I was offered by some ELN members. They assisted me by giving me money, and that way, in a short period of time I became a member. Suddenly, I was giving military instruction to some of the guys in the organization; they also started assigning me areas, among them Plan Los Foronda, which is next to the El Corazon neighborhood, and so I was in charge of other guys. As months went by, we were attacked and shot at several times from the El Corazon neighborhood by the paramilitary groups. They started shooting towards the Plan Los Foronda area and ended up wounding some civilians. We could not allow them to continue hurting the people in the area, so we used to fight back. I was in charge of military operations, and there were firefights at any moment. There were times when the whole area was being hit, but you could not even figure out where the shots were coming from. O several occasions, we found corpses lying on the streets but they were not victims of executions; they had been hit by stray bullets. These bullets could have been fired by us, the FARC, the CAP, the Paramilitary groups, or even the government forces. It became so bad, that we had to remove the street lights in the Plan Los Foronda area, so that people could walk around without getting shot at from the areas nearby.

It is well known that only 20% of the population had jobs, so the other 80% remained inside the area most of the time, since they did not have to leave to go to work. The area was extremely overpopulated, because even the 14, 15 and 16 year-old girls already had kids, and there were women who had more than seven kids. Kids looked unhealthy, with their bellybuttons popping out; full of parasites, and that was quite hard for us to see. All we could do was to prevent robberies, and girls or women being raped. However, when you are a member of an illegal armed group, whether it is called the ELN, FARC, People's Armed Commandoes, or whatever, you did not get there by mistake, it was because you knew that there you would get political indoctrination and you knew that you had to use the weapons they gave you. You should not have to, but either way, you do.

Many people thought well of me, because I would not allow anyone to be unjustly killed. I thought that whoever was using drugs did not deserve to die; someone just had to talk to him. I was not interested in doing executions. There were times when I was present when they happened, but that was because it was something I could not avoid. Either way, I was involved in the conflict as a member of an armed group, and those were things that sometimes happened. I would see two or three guys coming down with another, and five minutes later that other guy was already dead. Those people used to get executed because they were starting to affect the community by stealing in the area. For example, Ms. Pepa would go to the group and would say: 'Look, that guy robbed me yesterday, fifteen days ago he stole from me too and now he also stole my television; he also left me without a blender'. Then we would walk by and see the guy smoking some crack, getting high right in front of the kids. We would say to him 'go smoke that shit somewhere else', and he would respond 'you guys do not fuck with me, things are as they are', and would pull out a knife or revolver. Therefore, that is why more than one of those deaths was justified. I also know that there were many innocent people executed and I could not prevent that from happening. If I had been there, I am sure it would not have happened because I knew they were working people. That happened to a girl who was six months pregnant at the time. She worked in the El Carmen de Viboral village near Medellín city, where there were people from the Carlos Alirio Front. One of them was a guy they called 'Boy', who is now dead. He went to the house she lived in and dragged her out, because supposedly she was giving the paramilitary groups information on the people of El Carmen de Viboral. When I was told that they had executed her, I got really angry and asked why they had killed her. I told them that if she had been a snitch, she would have already turned many of us in, including me, whom she knew personally.

Authorities did not go inside Comuna 13, so the area became important because, for example, if in the El Catatumbo region located in the Eastern part of Colombia, someone had been wounded, they would send him to the comuna where he would be protected. The same thing would happen to those who had warrants for their arrest. If someone was kidnapped, that is where they would end up. If there was a weapons transaction taking place that is where it would be done. For this reason the area was of strategic importance. It was good for any type of situation.

With the intention of starting a new life, not involving violence, I retired from the ELN in December 2001, and started working as a security guard in the area near the Stadium. I moved with my wife and daughter to the Santa Monica neighborhood. I was living there for several months before I found out that there was a warrant for my arrest, for the crime of rebellion and supposedly also for terrorism, so I made the decision to take my family back to the Villa Laura neighborhood, the place I had left months ago. Once there, the organization put me back in charge of the Plan Los Foronda sector.

The CAP groups were more of our allies when it came to fighting in the area than were those of the FARC, because the latter wanted to control us. When the government forces would eventually go into the area, each group had to be responsible for its territory and 'Ugly Betty', the nickname used for the Police Armored Personnel Carrier, would get the worst of it because most of the shots were directed towards it.

We knew that one day, when we least expected it, all would be lost. The government would launch a military operation, and that was exactly what happened the day that the military operation Orion began. That 16th of October there was a lot of movement of troops and equipment in the area. I got up, and I was able to see from there, that it was the Army. All of a sudden, I heard several shots coming from behind where I was, and it so happened that the guys who were standing guard had started shooting at the soldiers who were in the lower part of the area. That day, wherever you turned you could hear shooting going on. I started going down the steps with two other guys, one with a shotgun and the other with a rifle. As I was walking I got shot in the shoulder, but I continued on my way down. The two guys that were with me got killed. One of them got shot in the face and the other in the neck. One of those guys had only been a member of the organization for 15 days and was 16 years old. I kept going down and hearing the buzzing sound of bullets passing near me. I went to the El Salado neighborhood, where one of the girl members of the organization stitched up my wound and let me stay there for four days. After that I went out, passed through all the check points and nobody stopped me. There were cops everywhere, but no one turned me in, no-one said 'that is Corolo', and that is how it was until the day the police arrested me.

It happened a night when I went to stay over at a house in the Ocho de Marzo neighborhood and someone found out and informed the authorities that I would be there, so the police went there to arrest me. When the police came into the house there was a guy named Juan David who was wounded and they found a gun he had to protect himself. They did not find anything on me, but I was the reason they were there in the first place, to execute the arrest warrant. They asked for me and for El Chata directly. They called out to me: 'Corolo, we know you are in there, pass us the beeper and your military identification'.

When you are a member of the organization, as a human being you fear death; but when you are in the middle of a shootout and you feel a bullet passing near you, one that was probably supposed to hit you, the fear disappears. My only fear was jail because I think death is better than being locked up in one of those places. Three days after being arrested by the police, my wife was assassinated on the road to the Santa Elena District in retaliation against me. Maybe it was done by the same people who turned me in. After I recovered my freedom from jail, the only thing I could do was stay in the city as long as possible, because my daughter was there and I needed to change and move ahead for her".

Some members of the illegal armed groups justified their joining and direct participation in the conflict with the argument of wanting to improve their neighborhood, which had become unsafe because it lacked employment opportunities and also because residents of these areas lived in extreme poverty. That is why -they said- they were easily persuaded to join the urban guerilla and paramilitary groups.

Gabriel*, a resident of Comuna 13, lived in the Antonio Nariño neighborhood with his girlfriend and two children. He was a member of the Paramilitary's Cacique Nutibara group in the area and later abandoned that lifestyle to take part in the Municipal Government's plan to help former combatants return to civilian life. He narrates the causes that drove him to join that illegal organization:

---

* Name changed to protect his identity.

"I decided to join the paramilitary group for many reasons: the constant harassment by the guerillas and especially all the unjustified deaths. It was not fair to have to walk the streets fearing that someone could shoot you, kidnap you or kill you. I was tired of so much abuse and of not being able to relax. Waking up to the sound of shooting used to be very hard, just like seeing how people were being killed by the rebels. It looked like a really dark future for our kids. There was no point acting as if you did not know what was going on in the area; it was not fair for us or for the other people. We used to use weapons because the situation was getting out of control; it was something no one could control, not even the authorities. We did not want to see any more violence, it was not logical to allow the rebels to do whatever they wanted. What we did was defend our sector. Our objective was to get rid of the guerillas as well as the thieves, so that people could walk to the corner without having to worry about something happening to them or having someone rob them and take their money.

Although I was involved in something bad, I used to do it for everyone's safety, not so much for me, but for my family. I knew I was exposing myself to being killed at any moment, but I used to do it so that my family could live in peace, so that in the future they could walk around the whole comuna without the fear of running into an illegal checkpoint set up by the guerillas, where they would be kidnapped or killed. Our mission in the organization was to take care of the neighborhood, carry out operations against the rebels and control thieves and junkies, because it was not logical either to allow junkies to take over the area. We did this so that when our kids went outside to play on the street, they would not see groups of teenagers hanging out on the corner, smoking marijuana, or using other types of drugs. These were the priorities of the organization. If these teenagers did not understand that they could not rob or do other bad things against the community, and then just lost control, it was their decision to die.

159

On November 24th, 2003 I turned myself in along with other members and signed up for the municipal government's reinsertion plan. We did this because we saw that things had changed a lot in the area, and people were able to live in peace. Now my expectations are to be able to finish school, see my kids grow up and provide for my family's needs".

The military operation Orion

Luis Pérez Gutiérrez, the Mayor of Medellín City, from 2000 to 2003, narrates:

"There are many problems of law and order in the country which the government and private sectors try to ignore, or try to cover up to make the community believe that such problems do not exist. The conflict in Comuna 13 is one of those problems that the government of Antioquia tried to cover up for many years. It is said that the FARC, ELN, CAP and the AUC had been there for many years and the problem had been ignored because no one was willing to deal with it. That is why it became a social cancer for Medellín and the whole metropolitan area and a paradise for all those who wanted to carry out their criminal activities here. They used to plan and prepare crimes throughout the entire city in that area, with total impunity. The people in the zone were practically held hostage.

When I became the Mayor of Medellín City, I started to worry about this. My administration as well as the one before me, which Juan Gomez Martinez presided over, had carried out some infrastructural work in the area, so I made the decision of going to inaugurate those sites because it was pretty humiliating for a mayor to try to understand that there are certain areas in the city where authorities cannot get in to do their job. So I requested several members of the government forces to visit the area with me, even though they insisted that it was very dangerous. It is very painful to admit that in such an important city as Medellín, there was a neighborhood minutes away from downtown which could not be visited by authorities. It is something I find degrading; I also think that allowing that to go on is an act of irresponsibility on the part of any leader.

On May 30th, 2002, we decided to go to the area along with several journalists. I was calm because I have always been confident that our government security forces are capable of resolving any of the problems posed by criminals. When we were about to get there, the bus in which I was traveling with the journalists was attacked, and bullets hit a car from the Transportation Department which was moving in front of us. It was immobilized by the bullets and was left stranded in the middle of the road, so we could not progress. All of us who were on the bus crouched down and I covered myself with a bullet proof vest. Amidst the shooting the driver in a very agile way and still crouching, put the bus in reverse and was able to get it out of there to a safe place, where we were not in danger anymore.

It was a very scary situation but at the same time, educational for a leader because that is when you are able to understand the pain that the population must endure and the fear that the shootings fill you with. I thought that if this could happen to a mayor who is somewhat protected, how would it be for a citizen who cannot hire bodyguards. On that day I asked General Gallego as well as General Montoya, to initiate actions to take back Comuna 13 or else we would all have to resign; I could not believe that generals and elected mayors were scared of the urban gangs which were multiplying their violence throughout the metropolitan area of El Valle de Aburrá.

We started preparing to take back Comuna 13. Some prior attempts had already failed to take it back because when the police would start to make their way up, they were pushed back with strong fire power. The first thing we did was to design maps of all access points to the streets of Comuna 13, because all the traffic and direction information signs had been destroyed. I also asked for a police station to be built in the area, and it was approved with City Hall's budget. People would not feel safe until they saw government security forces permanently in the comuna. After some difficulties with plotting the terrain, topographers were sent to the area to measure slopes and to be able to make accurate designs of maps. These topographers were usually fired upon and thrown out of the area, so they had to go back later on under extreme protection in order to do their job.

On October 14th, 2002, when the conflict became worse, bullets reached an apartment in the Santa Monica neighborhood where a doctor friend of mine lived with his only daughter who was a student at the University of Antioquia. His daughter was struck and killed by a bullet when she was standing near her window. I went to the funeral home, and saw the girl's father, who was very sad. I had never seen a man as depressed as he was. I could not really stay too long because the pain of seeing my friend's suffering was unbearable. When I was leaving the funeral home, a man who was also crying stopped me and told me that his son, who was a student at EAFIT University, had also been killed by a stray bullet. That made it two young university students, uninvolved in the conflict, who had been brutally killed.

I could see that the government forces were unable to resolve the conflict, so I called President Uribe and I told him that the situation that the city was experiencing was unbearable, and if he did not help me resolve this problem, I would consider myself to have failed the city, because I was making them believe that they had a Mayor who was capable of solving the situation. The President was very worried.

At about three in the afternoon, I got a call from General Ospina who told me that the President had called him to put himself at my disposal. We met the same day and agreed to take charge of the situation. He said that in three days he would bring five hundred men who were specialized in urban terrorism, and that in alliance with the Metropolitan Police and the Army´s Fourth Brigade, we could execute a plan to take back Comuna 13. Some people who had pending arrest warrants from the District Attorney´s Office had already been identified. We all made the decision that even if taking back the comuna took one month or one year, we would not retreat from the area".

General Mario Montoya Uribe was the Commander of the Army´s Fourth Brigade, with headquarters in Medellín city, at the time of the worsening of the conflict in Comuna 13 and during Operation Orion. Montoya says:

"For many years illegal armed groups had executed a political project in Comuna 13, which consisted of taking the place of legal authorities to impose their own authority in the area. They restricted movement of people and groceries, imposed their own way of life, extorted shopkeepers, taxi drivers, and businesses in general, and killed whoever they wanted. The Government had lost its authority in the area, and government forces had to stop their military operations when seeing that the civilian population could be in danger".

On October 16th, 2002, government security forces launched Operation Orion. It was called Orion because the Army is used to assigning names to their military operations, which relate to the first letter of the month they take place in, according to General Mario Montoya.

More than 1200 men from the Army, Police, DAS (Administrative Security Department), CTI (Technical Investigation Unit), Air Force and Marines participated in Operation Orion. They were supervised by Human Rights institutions.

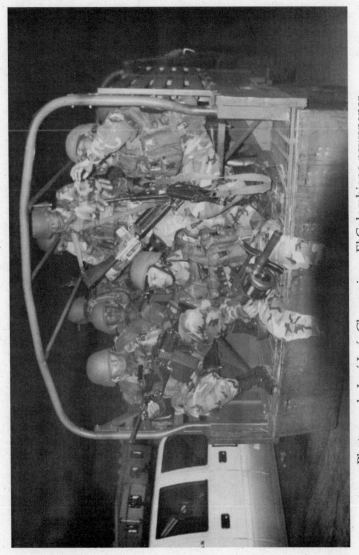

Photograph: José Luís Chavarriaga, El Colombiano newspaper.

These troops got to the area at approximately 1:00 in the morning, and started their advance in the La Torre sector of Belencito, La Gallera sector of Nuevos Conquistadores, Veinte de Julio and El Salado neighborhoods. The troops knew that the illegal armed groups had 30 trenches from which they had ample control of the area 24 hours a day and in which there were some snipers positioned. In each trench they had a rifle and a carbine, a communication radio, and grenades or handmade explosive devices. They also had AK-47 rifles, R15s, G3s, carbines with telescopic sites, Uzi machineguns, shotguns, pistols, revolvers, M-60 machine guns, M-79 grenade launchers and some antipersonnel mines.

When they noticed the presence of the government forces, the rebels opened fire and a hell of a lot of shots broke loose in the area. A short time later, Marine Lieutenant Mario Alonso Villegas García and soldiers Juan Carlos López and Johnny Enrique Álvarez died in the confrontations.

The military operation that would split the history of Comuna 13 in two was taking place. The armed confrontation lasted until the afternoon, although the echo of the shooting and crying of tens of people frightened by the long combat was still heard on the mountainside for many hours.

Metropolitan Police Sergeant Felipe*, who participated in the Orion Operation, narrates the moments of tension he lived through with the other police officers he was with, and the drama of his 21-year-old friend Second Lieutenant Diego Andrés Acosta Herrera's death. He died when they were trying to accomplish their mission of getting into some of the places where the guerilla groups were entrenched with the use of their armored vehicle:

"I had been previously given the order of taking the armored vehicle called the Panther, along with Second Lieutenant

---

* Name changed to protect his identity.

Acosta Herrera, a captain, a sergeant and four more officers. Second Lieutenant Acosta was looking through the front window of the vehicle; I was near him and the other officers placed themselves on the inside near the walls. At approximately 7:30 in the morning we went to the Veinte de Julio neighborhood, where there were a lot of heavily armed FARC, ELN and CAP rebel members fighting the Army and the anti-guerilla unit of the Antioquia Police Department. The last group was unable to advance towards where the rebels were because the combat was intense. Our objective was to open a path and clear the area so the unit could advance. The first goal was to clear the urban guerilla from the Veinte de Julio neighborhood which we accomplished by: destroying their trenches, capturing some guerilla members and seizing their weapons, among which we found a carbine with a telescopic sight.

At 09:00 in the morning, when we already had control over the neighborhood, we tried to advance to the reservoir in sector 2 of La Independencia, not too far from where we were. As we attempted to ascend the hill, the insurgents attacked us with hand grenades and we had to go back twice to reconsider our strategy and avoid human casualties. Later we tried going up again, and amidst the crossfire and explosions, we made it. Then several police officers and soldiers got there. They stayed in that position and we continued uphill in the vehicle with some difficulty because there was still a lot of shooting. It was approximately 10:30 in the morning when we got to a place where there were four dead guerilla members with their long range weapons lying next to them.

In the middle of the confrontation, a rebel fired a grenade round towards us and it struck right outside the front window. Inside we heard a loud bang and saw the flash; Second Lieutenant Acosta immediately fell wounded on top of me. I had also been wounded in the face and I was very stunned, but not as badly as he was. I tried to make him feel better and keep his spirits up, although I knew he was going to die. It took us fifteen minutes to get down from where we were to the El Salón Rojo sector, because we did not have any side view mirrors anymore and the hill we were on was very steep. When we got there, we immediately put Acosta in another vehicle and he was quickly taken to hospital, but he died there at approximately 2:00 in the afternoon.

The rest of the police officers who were in the armored vehicle stayed in the area, afterwards we went up the steps on foot along with the Police Gaula Anti Kidnapping Group and the Elite Anti-Terrorism Group. At about 11:45 in the morning, we were able to free two people who had been kidnapped and were being held for ransom. The combats did not stop; the rebels had withdrawn to the Cuatro Esquinas sector and Pedro J. Gomez School in the El Salado neighborhood, where they were still resisting government forces.

In the afternoon we found an AK-47 rifle with lots of ammunition. That day we stayed in the area all night, maximizing security measures. The next day, October 17th, at about 6:30 in the morning, we started enforcing some search warrants with the DAS. Then we captured a man and found an underground stash where there were two AK-47 rifles, a Winchester shotgun, an Uzi machinegun, several grenades, communication radios, ammo vests and camouflage uniforms. The search warrants were served all day, and there were several kidnap victims freed. We also captured some criminals and seized a lot of weapons, explosives and bombs.

At about 6:00 in the afternoon they ordered all police officers in the area to be relieved. I was taken to the clinic because of the wounds I had, where they diagnosed a hearing impairment. As time passed my wounds healed but the experiences will never leave my mind. They will always be there, to remind me of the 16th of October, 2002, when the biggest trauma for me was the death of my friend, Second Lieutenant Acosta".

Balance of this military operation

During the Orion Operation, the Sijin anti-explosives group of the police defused a bus loaded with dynamite and shrapnel that had been left on a street of the El Salado neighborhood by the guerilla members. The Sijin also carried out controlled detonations for several fragmentation grenades which had been thrown by the illegal armed groups but had not exploded and were found on the ground without their safety pins. Government forces rescued 21 kidnap victims and seized 330 kilos of explosives, 90 grenades, 62 firearms, 6,452 rounds of ammunition of different calibers, two kilos of potassium chloride and several handmade explosive devices. Many people were also captured.

According to Brigadier General José Leonardo Gallego Castrillón, who was the commander of the El Valle de Aburra Metropolitan Police when the Orion Operation took place, "The intervention in Comuna 13 originated in the great need and evident urgency of getting all the institutions and logistical means necessary to intervene into the area affected for so many years by the actions of illegal armed groups. There was not only the need to appropriate the area, the terrain, but also of carrying out an indispensable plan to favor the population, at the mercy of these illegal factions. Specific interventions were carried out in order to reestablish the presence of the Government and to get rid of the originating factors of violence, to be able to allow government institutions to go in and do their work".

Unfortunately, in carrying out the Orion Operation there were some casualties, 18 in total: four civilians, four members of the government forces and ten alleged members of urban guerillas. There were also 34 wounded: 14 members of the government forces and another 20, amongst which were civilians and guerilla members.

Adriana María Mazo is a resident of the Las Independencias neighborhood. Despite the conflict that took place in the area, she had a "normal" life. At 22 years old she lived with her parents, her five siblings and young daughter who at the time of the Orion Operation was eight months old. Adriana Maria narrates her experience:

"My life took a total turn on October 16th, 2002. That day, a lot of shooting were heard early in the morning. At approximately six o'clock, I took the risk of leaving with the intention of going to work. After departing from my house and walking for two blocks, I ran into several armed gunmen who told me that I could not continue on my way, so I immediately turned back; that was when I heard a shot and felt a strong impact on my neck. I had gotten struck by a bullet that went out the right side of my shoulder. I fell to the ground, face down. I tried to get up, but did not have any strength. I was able to observe that I was losing blood slowly; I was making a huge effort to ask for help, but no one dared to help me for fear of being shot themselves. About 45 minutes went by. I was still on the floor and had lost a lot of blood. A lady, who knew me, saw me wounded on the ground and went to alert my family. Soon, my aunt Margarita and my cousin Wilber got there; they could not stop themselves from crying seeing me in such a condition. My cousin lifted me up in his arms to take me to the aid center but, since he could still hear a lot of shooting, he threw me over his shoulder so he could run easier until we got to where he was able to put me inside a vehicle which took me to the medical center at the San Javier neighborhood. When the doctor saw my condition he sent me to the San Vicente de Paúl Hospital, in the center of the city. There they made a great effort to keep me alive. I was unconscious for three days. I got a little worse and was in critical condition for five days. I felt a lot of pain on my left shoulder and on my face.

After being at the hospital for two weeks, a doctor approached me and asked how I felt. I asked him why I could not feel my legs and my left hand; he told me that I had suffered a severe wound to the spinal cord which had affected my limbs and deprived me of movement in them. It was really hard for me to hear that, as it affected me a lot emotionally.

After two more weeks, I was taken to a house that my family had rented in another neighborhood of the city because I was really impaired psychologically and did not want to keep living in the neighborhood where I had been wounded.

It has been very hard for me to get used to the idea of being disabled, of not being able to move my legs and my left arm. I have cried a lot because of my disability and even more when I see my little girl growing up, without being able at least to play with her. Seeing myself forced to have other people do everything for me is very frustrating. However, my family, friends and people who came to give me hope, helped me a lot with facing this unpleasant situation. A while back I got some good news: the doctor told me that it was possible to get the movement back in my left arm with surgery. I try to stay calm, with the hope of someday being able to recover me a little".

Conflict Trails

"Bullet-riddled homes, destroyed doors, bullet holes from short and long range weapons had been left as testimony of an urban war, for some without precedent in the history of the city".[41]

After the Orion Operation, authorities positioned themselves in Comuna 13. Most of the members of illegal armed groups who were not captured by the authorities left the area.

Luis Pérez Gutiérrez states: "Once the comuna had been taken back, people's happiness showed in their faces because, although we had not given them any material things, we had given them their freedom back. Even though they did not have jobs or maybe were starving, they had been released from their slavery. When I saw the dazzling happiness of those people, it filled me with satisfaction.

I would like to add that our purpose was not only military, but also civil in nature. That is why, after the military operation we sent the necessary resources into the area in order to recuperate schools and give work to the people. From that time on, murders and crime rates in the city decreased and the peace that is enjoyed in Medellín owes itself, to a great extent, to the Comuna 13 intervention. Thanks to that intervention

---

[41] Esparza, Catalina. "The tension in Comuna 13 decreases". In: BBC World, Latin America, October 20th, 2002.

by government forces, criminals in different comunas in the city have noticed that they cannot mess with the police.

Comuna 13 is an example for the whole country, which taught us that there are crime hot spots in different cities from where the violence experienced nowadays is expanding".

For his part, Ricardo Aricapa reminds us:

"After the end of the war, the Municipal Government promoted a special investment plan with coverage throughout the entire Comuna 13 to consolidate pacification, stimulate the economy, restore social networks and pay part of the city's historical debt to this marginalized area. It was a plan that included fixing damages, building infrastructure, intervention in public spaces and improvements to some basic public services. Up to December 2003, this plan had garnered investments of thirty-eight thousand million pesos [Equivalent to approximately $13 Million USD at the time]. That was the amount that the different state municipal entities had separated from their normal budgets which was quite a large amount if compared to the normal investment the Municipality allocates to marginalized areas.

However, some community non-government organization leaders that have tracked the process have said that it all came down to a bunch of emergency investment actions to solve specific problems and immediate needs and thus, with barely accurate and short-lived effects".[42]

At the same time, Mr. Rubén Darío Restrepo, from the La Loma sector working group has stated that "[...] the multiple needs of the community make investments seem small".[43]

---

[42] Aricapa, Ricardo. Comuna 13: Chronicles of an urban war, Second Edition, Universidad de Antioquia Editorial, Medellín, 2005, p. 235.

[43] El Colombiano. "More training for Comuna 13". November 22nd, 2002. p. 11A.

It is important to remember that "Programs aimed at providing immediate attention to the crisis must be part of prolonged structural programs, planned for mid and long-term, so that the first -short term- actions do not end up being provisional and temporary".[44]

In the words of priest Mario Castrillón Restrepo, "This continues being an area that needs more investment in people. Although it is true that they now have good public services, a good sewer system and telephone network, the biggest scourge for many families here is hunger. They need investment in jobs, education and alternatives for youth, many of whom are leaders who are willing to transform that reality into another one in which values and peace can be experienced".

Overcoming the crisis

After Operation Orion, many teachers from the comuna received psychological help and training directed by the Department of Education. After that, they continued teaching students about respect for life and tolerance. They developed several educational projects such as building a culture of legality in which students are taught the importance of the Rule of Law in a Social State and defense of its laws. They also designed some modules in which concepts of peace and coexistence were the main focus. The workshops designed by students from different subjects had one thing in common: they all had positive messages. Teachers used to positively reinforce students every time they excelled in something, with applauses, accolades or small gifts. There were many fun and recreational activities in which parents got involved and even helped teachers with the younger children.

---

[44] Socioeconomic Diagnosis of Comuna 13 Report, Universidad Autónoma Latinoamericana and Empresas Públicas de Medellín. October, 2002.

As time has passed, teenagers have had learning experiences that make them stronger and help them overcome the traumas suffered through the conflict.

On the other hand, the Metropolitan Police sent a group of community police officers to the area to be in charge of helping build a secure and peaceful culture through social programs, actions and strategies that would create a joint venture made up of community, municipal government, and police. Through the Youth Civic Police Program, the Community Police have gotten many children from Comuna 13 together to teach them about domestic violence, drug use, and alcoholism prevention. It is a preventive program, which aims to generate discipline, teach kids about values and integrate them with kids from the neighborhoods nearby through games and different types of activities, directed by the police officers who participate in the program.

Using the DARE (Drug Abuse Resistance Education) program, the Community Police trained kids from the Monseñor Perdomo, Pío XII, Veinte de Julio, El Corazón and Betania educational institutions. The training lasted one hour per week for six months and they were taught about how to avoid using drugs and reject violence. After the training they all got a certificate.

The community Police have also been developing community security programs in the area, such as a local neighborhood watch, which consists of getting residents together to help them involve themselves in the security of their area; additionally citizen safety schools, which consists of training groups of people in topics related to peaceful coexistence, citizen security, urbanity, and institutional knowledge, among other subjects and preventive type programs.

"Causative" factors and other challenges

"The National Institution for Further Training (.
emphasizes that the presence of armed delinquents and t.
murder rate in the city are more serious in sectors where
public space is limited, poverty and unemployment are
noticeably higher, education and housing are less available,
and access to the formal justice system is more difficult to
obtain. In other words, where there are clearer signs of social
inequality and limited opportunities."[45]

During the period in which the civil conflict in Comuna 13
took its course, poverty was a visible factor in the communal
existence of the neighbourhood. Most people struggled
every day to cover their most basic needs. Such was the life
of Albeiro, a resident of La Torre in Belencito, who had few
professional opportunities, and therefore struggled to survive
with his wife and small daughter. Every day he went out
looking for something in building work or deliveries, since
he didn't have the qualifications for anything else. He and
his small family were known as the denizens of the floating
house, because the box of wood they lived in projected over
the edge of a precipice, and was held up by sticks. Walking
inside it made the floor tremble, and the balcony was unsafe,
because it could have broken off at any moment and plunged
into the gaping void beneath.

While the civil conflict gathered pace, Albeiro did not have
resources to spend on his daughter's studies, and his future
hung by a thread. Sometimes they only had one meal a day
or went through the whole day by drinking raw cane sugar
water. With the passing of time, one of his daughters died,
owing to a combination of illness and hunger. It was as if

---

[45] Jiménez Morales, Germán. "The violence in Medellín is equivalent to
eliminating a municipality from the map". In: El Colombiano, May 6th,
2002. p. 10A

fate were opposed to Albeiro and his loved ones. In other parts of the same city, there were people living in the lap of luxury, but in this area, there were others, like Albeiro, who had nothing at all to take home. For him, survival was more of a challenge than just lying down and dying would have been.

Yet every day, he made an effort to get ahead somehow, and at least take a piece of bread home to his family.

It is important to remember that there were parts of the city that required State investment not merely in the sense of public safety through crime prevention, but also through social projects aimed at satisfying citizens' basic needs. "For the Medellín Ombudsman*, if public safety were understood purely in terms of police presence, this would signify that the State had become profoundly weak and deprived of able and efficient institutions equipped to channel inclusion to the most disadvantaged members of society, according to the pattern projected for a lawful social state."[46]

The void and poverty left in this part of the city by the institutions of the state were taken advantage of by the different armed groups of an illegal nature that participated in the civil conflict at national level (the CAP, on the other hand, operated solely in the thirteenth Comuna).

The outcome was that all these groups saw the slopes of Comuna 13 as ripe pickings for their own interests, taking advantage of the situation to recruit young people through their offer of entirely mendacious opportunities. "The guerilla groups, and in reaction the paramilitary groups, tend to settle

---

*   Government Institution whose mission is the promotion and defense of the rights of individuals, monitoring official conduct and governance, and the protection of public interest, amongst others.

[46]   Report and article about Human Rights by the Personería de Medellín. 2002

into territories that have high and persistent crime rates, where they can offer residents some type of safety, which sometimes residents accept despite its high intrinsic costs".[47]

"Today, a programme of State intervention in conflict zones is necessary, especially ones like Comuna 13 which need investment, mediation and participative strategies."[48]

According to psychologist Ángela Quintero López, who was a teacher in Educational Institution Las Independencias, "The challenge is to create escape routes from this situation for people which imply economic and political solutions, which make them safe and which help to reorder the social fabric, empower social institutions, psychosocial support of a community nature and psychotherapeutic support for victims.

In Colombia, and particularly in Comuna 13 of the Municipality of Medellín, we face the following challenges:

- Revaluating physical, psychic, social and spiritual life
- Reconstructing trustable social bonds
- Fortifying human dignity
- Reducing the gap between those who have everything, or at least a lot, and those who have nothing, or at least, very little."[49]

The job is just beginning for authorities, who at least have made the effort of investing in human and structural development

---

[47] Salazar, Alonso. "War in the streets". In: SEMANA Magazine, Edition No. 1.077, December 23rd, 2002.

[48] Socioeconomic Diagnosis of Comuna 13 Report, Universidad Autonoma Latinoamericana and Empresas Públicas de Medellín. October, 2002.

[49] Document: "The effects of war on boys, girls and teenagers". Psychologist Angela Quintero Lopez, a teacher at Las Independencias Educational Institution, 2002.

in the sector, keeping the peace, and wiping out threats and also the sense of threat in local residents.

Nevertheless, it is still an important priority for the community to use any means it has to let authorities know of situations that these may not yet be aware of, such as deteriorating social conditions, risk-associated health conditions, dangerous structures, elements that generate lack of safety, or the reappearance of armed delinquents in the Comuna who might potentially limit residents' exercise of their citizens' rights.

Why did I want to write this book?

By the end of 2003, I was assigned to work in Medellin's Comuna 13 as a member of a community police group in the sector, with the mission of carrying out social work and building trust in the community towards the police. This had to do with accomplishing integration activities, managing essential resources for the residents who most needed it through governmental and private entities, the voluntary disarmament of residents of the sector who had weapons in their possession, and the symbolic disarmament of students within the schools in which they gave the police their war toy guns, in exchange for soccer balls, dolls and toy cars. In this process, with some children and other young people, the police received real weapons, ammunition or explosives that were found in the streets, many of them lost by members of the illegal armed groups that were present in the area, and other ones had been kept at different homes by residents of the sector before the end of the armed conflict.

While I worked there, many residents of the area told me stories about what they had lived or witnessed during the armed conflict; many of them seemed incredible to me, my mind could not assimilate situations that were so critical for the community had appeared in the Comuna 13 of Medellin, stories that seemed fantastic because reality in many cases exceeded fiction.

Due to so many stories they told me, I asked members of the community if there was already a documentary or a book telling what happened; however, they all said no; but then they kept telling me new stories daily to the point that I got obsessed with finding out new details about that armed conflict. After someone told me one of his experiences, we mentioned that so far, no one had written a book about what was happening, and as a joke, I said, "I will have to do it."

The days were passing by while those words, "I will have to do it" resounded in my mind until they turned into "I will do it." So strong was my motivation to write the book that not even difficulties mattered to me. I started reading journalism books to reinforce my literary abilities. Also, day after day, as people told me their stories, I asked for permission to write the accounts and to gather the information.

After that, I began to type and classify the diverse stories according to the topic of each one: those relating to children in armed groups, kidnappings, and so on, until I organized the book over the course of four years. In short, I had so much desire to read a book about what had happened in the Comuna 13 that, although it did not exist yet, I found it necessary to write it in order to be able to read it. I also want other people to know this story to remind the victims of that tragic past where human suffering was evidenced, and to avoid in some way that the violent acts described in this book can be repeated anywhere in the world.

The social and cultural transformation in Comuna 13

At this moment, Comuna 13 is a site of profound social and cultural transformation, whose inhabitants have progressed beyond the crises which caused them so many problems. In the process of implementing this change, they have been supported by the government and some private sector investment. The Mayoralty of Medellín has provided the zone with new means of transport, including a cable car, known in the city as "Cable Metro." This links up Comuna 13 to the metro system. A network of escalators has also been constructed, so that those who live in more secluded parts of the mountain may get home easily, without having to climb hundreds of stairs in narrow alleys.

A considerable number of artists and entrepreneurs from the thirteenth Comuna have contributed to the sector's development, displaying their talents through attractive paintings and graffiti all along the way. Many of these evoke nature and experiences of theirs mediated by artistic expression, which has already attracted thousands of international tourists into the area, who are frequently amazed at the innovative systems of transport, the beautiful paintings along the walkways, the young dancers, the handicraft artists, the candies and delicious coffee that they serve there. Above all, however, they are impressed by the immense cordiality and entrepreneurial spirit of the local people.